MY
REALITY

MY REALITY

MELISSA RYCROFT

GALLERY BOOKS

New York   London   Toronto   Sydney   New Delhi

Gallery Books
A Division of Simon & Schuster, Inc.
1230 Avenue of the Americas
New York, NY 10020

This work is a memoir. Events, actions, and experiences and their consequences over a period of years have been retold as the author presently recollects them. Some names and identifying characteristics have been changed, and some dialogue has been recreated from memory.

Photo insert credits:
Page 1: Natalie Woods; page 2: Natalie Woods (top), Daniel Costilla (bottom); page 3: Robin DeHoyos (top), Ashley Smith (bottom); page 4: Tye Strickland (bottom); page 5: Michelle Mix; page 8: Laura Parker (top left). All other photos courtesy of the author.

First Gallery Books hardcover edition June 2012

GALLERY BOOKS and colophon are registered trademarks of Simon & Schuster, Inc.

For information about special discounts for bulk purchases, please contact Simon & Schuster Special Sales at 1-866-506-1949 or business@simonandschuster.com.

The Simon & Schuster Speakers Bureau can bring authors to your live event. For more information or to book an event, contact the Simon & Schuster Speakers Bureau at 1-866-248-3049 or visit our website at www.simonspeakers.com.

Designed by Jaime Putorti

Manufactured in the United States of America

10   9   8   7   6   5   4   3   2   1

Library of Congress Cataloging-in-Publication Data

Rycroft, Melissa.
  My reality / Melissa Rycroft. — 1st Gallery
Books hardcover ed.
      p.   cm.
    1. Rycroft, Melissa   2. Television personalities—United
States—Biography.   3. Celebrities—United States—Biography.   I. Title.
    PN1992.4.S793A3   2011
    791.4502'8092—dc22
    [B]
                                  2011012506

ISBN 978-1-4516-3164-7

This is dedicated to the newest love of my life:
my daughter, Ava.
Looking at her makes everything that's happened
on my journey to finding love absolutely worth it.
She's the epitome of my happiness,
and I would go on this whole crazy, heartbreaking
journey again, if she were the outcome.
I love you, Ava Grace.

CONTENTS

PROLOGUE

’m the girl who gets her heart broken. I don’t know what it is about me, but that’s how it’s always been. And, let’s be honest, that’s how a lot of people still know me.

I guess I shouldn’t be surprised. The entire world watched what it assumed was me getting my heart smashed on TV’s *The Bachelor*. All of my previous relationships ended almost as badly. Call me unlucky, not the relationship type, or just not the *sustainable-relationship* type—whatever it was, I definitely was not good at the dating game.

So I was totally surprised when people started coming up to me after *The Bachelor* to ask me for romantic advice. I couldn’t figure out why in the world they’d want help from the girl who historically *never* got the guy. Sure, my dating life has a happy ending now, and I’m married to a man who is my soul mate and best friend, but a lot of people don’t know that. Some people who do know still can’t picture me with anyone but Jason Mesnick. And, again, we all know how well that ended—or at least appeared to end, which I’ll get to in a bit.

But then it clicked: People weren't after the secrets of a successful relationship (if they were, I'd have to direct them to someone more qualified to help!), they were looking for advice on what to do when things *DON'T* work out. And that's a subject I definitely know something about.

Maybe reading my story can stop some of you out there from doing the same things I did wrong. Most of all, I lost my sense of self. And I do know, without a doubt, that I had to finally find my real and true self before I could ever be in a healthy relationship. I think the same is probably true for everyone else.

Of course, the problem is that lovesick people aren't much for taking advice. I know that better than anyone. I look back at the girl I used to be, and I can't help laughing at her: *You are making every mistake in the book, girl. You are doing everything wrong. It almost seems like you are TRYING to ruin this relationship. Why not just hand him your heart and a hammer?*

But I couldn't see the truth back then.

People who watched *The Bachelor* think they know what I went through on the show and during its aftermath. Because it's called a reality TV show, they assume it's the real story. But the reality that people saw was *not* the reality of my life—or even of the show! Actually, I've gone through a ton more, some worse than what you've seen, and some better.

As I've always said, the best writers in the world couldn't have dreamed up my story; it's too unbelievable. That's why I'm finally ready to tell it like it really was. By sharing my reality with all of you, maybe—just maybe—it'll help those of you out there to avoid, or at least get over, the kind of soul crushing heartbreaks I endured. Because if I could spare you from the kind of pain I went through, I certainly would.

MY
REALITY

One

·

MY WORST
BREAKUP EVER

As the girl who was always unlucky in love, I've got several breakup stories to choose from when it comes to finding that one defining moment—the one when you feel like you've hit the lowest of the low; the proverbial rock bottom. My *Bachelor* breakup may be my most famous and most humiliating romantic ordeal but it's not the worst one I've ever been through. Yes, there is actually something worse than having an engagement ring taken back by the man who gave it to you, while he tells you that he has feelings for another woman, who he's been talking to behind your back . . . *ALL* on national television.

By far, my worst breakup—the one that hurt the most and is also, literally, the reason I am who I am and where I am today—actually happened before I was even a contestant on *The Bachelor*.

It took place in March 2008, just shy of my twenty-fifth birthday. It started out like most breakups do. Whether they're the ones we've experienced ourselves, or the ones we've seen in a million romantic comedies, the problem always seems to be the same: There's a big—and I mean a *BIG*—difference between the girl's point of view and the guy's point of view. And just guess who was more serious about the relationship in my case? Well, here's a clue: How many guys ever want to have *the talk*? Right.

I'd been dating my boyfriend, Tye Strickland, for about a year, and I had that gut feeling that he was *the one*. The problem was, *he* didn't know the same thing about me. In fact, he didn't seem to know whether he was that serious about dating me at all. I could sense this, and I was terrified of scaring him away. So when it came to talking about our relationship, we just didn't. We never had the talk about our status. I never pushed to take things further and never put any pressure on the relationship. I'd think, *Hey, if he wants to keep this light and casual—after a YEAR . . . I'm okay with that.*

Yeah. Sure I was.

I tried to be casual, even though I wasn't feeling that way. I really did.

Sometimes, I guess, it's just easier to be delusional than to face reality.

·

Things had been amazing at the start (as most relationships are at the beginning). He was so cute and sweet, and we had so much fun together. I'd always leave him smiling, which, for a girl, is the best sign that you've found someone great.

We had so much in common. When we met, one of the first things we noticed about each other was that we each wore a small cross around our necks as a symbol of our faith, which was very unusual in our circle of friends. We had both grown up in Dallas and were very close to our families. Our parents were still married, and we believed in the importance of making a lifetime commitment to someone when we were older (in Tye's case, WAY older). We saw our parents often (and brought each other home to meet our families fairly early on). We loved football, particularly the Dallas Cowboys. The fact that I was a Cowboys Cheerleader and that he had friends associated with the cheerleaders meant that much of our lives revolved around the games. We had similar senses of humor and could make each other laugh for hours. It was all going great.

And then, six months in, being a hopeless romantic, the inevitable happened: I fell in love with him. I didn't mean to. I actually didn't even know that I had at the time. It just . . . happened. And not only was he NOT in love with me, he didn't even know if he wanted a girlfriend. And, while I knew he really liked me, he was just fine fitting me into his busy schedule of working, working out, and hanging out—around the clock—with his group of completely inseparable (and, yes, single) buddies.

I didn't want to admit it—not to him and not to myself—but I wasn't getting what I needed. After several months of hanging on as best as I could, it finally hit me how deeply unhappy I was. As with most things, there was one clarifying moment that changed everything.

I literally remember it like it was yesterday. House of Blues had just opened a new venue in Dallas, and I had been talking for months about how much I wanted to go check it out. Tye kept telling me that we'd go together soon, since he knew how badly I wanted to go. It was definitely one date that I was looking forward to with him.

One Friday, I texted Tye from work, like I always did, and asked him what he was up to that night. At first, he gave me his typical answer: "I don't know yet." Shocking: He didn't have plans. He didn't ask what I was doing, which was also typical.

Now, from here, I know how bad this looks, so just bear with me for a minute. Not only had he not asked me out for a date that night, but he also still wouldn't commit to hanging out with me, even when he didn't have any other definite plans. In my warped little mind, as far as I was concerned, he hadn't said that he did *not* want to hang out with me, he'd just said that he didn't know what he was doing. Right? So there was still hope that we'd end up seeing each other before the night was through (especially if I just "happened" to end up where he was hanging out, which was my MO). I know, I know, but keep in mind that this is the *before* section of my story.

When I got done with work, I went out to dinner with some of my girlfriends who were fellow Dallas Cowboys Cheerleaders. It was a great night out with my friends, but I couldn't stop thinking about Tye and wondering what he was up to. So I sent him a text message:

"What are you doing?"

No response.

I waited for what seemed like an ample amount of time to send another text message. (Five minutes is ample time, right?)

"Where are you?"

Again, no response.

Hmmm . . .

Now, looking back, I know Tye's initial lack of response was a clear signal, but I couldn't resist sending the second text! *He's my flippin' boyfriend! Don't I have a right to ask what he's doing on a Friday night? And why doesn't he want to know what I'M doing? Heck, why doesn't he want to be with me right now?!?*

And then it happened. He texted back!

"I'm going to the House of Blues with the guys."

Are you kidding me??

I couldn't believe it! He had gone and made plans without me to do the ONE thing that he knew I REALLY wanted to do! Suddenly,

I felt my cheeks heat up and my heart begin to race as it hit me how little he cared, or even thought about my feelings . . . not just my feelings, but me!! And, just like that, after months of denial, I was finally mad. Not upset. Not bummed. Furious. I was done. I couldn't stand it anymore. I needed something to happen, good or bad. THAT NIGHT. And so I took matters into my own hands.

I sat through the rest of dinner, trying to act like everything was normal. But I was too busy formulating my plan of attack to pay attention to the conversation at the table. And the more time that passed, the angrier I got. A wonderful state of mind to be in when you're about to confront the person you love. . . .

When I left the restaurant, I didn't tell any of the girls where I was going or what I planned to do. I knew they would have tried to talk me out of it, and I didn't want anything to stand in my way. Not that there was anything that anybody could have said or done that would have stopped me anyhow. I was an irrational girl on a mission.

I went over to Tye's house. I knew I was pulling the psycho-girl move, even while I was doing it. But I had reached that point where I was way beyond any kind of rational discussion or thought. I guess that's why the word "psycho" applies.

I got to Tye's condo around midnight. He had given me a key because I was always in and out of there, and so I let myself in and waited for him to get home.

And I waited.

And I waited.

The more I waited, the angrier I got. I sat on his bed and listened for him to come in the door. I didn't call any of my girlfriends. I didn't pull out my makeup and primp. I just sat there quietly and waited to have my say. I was nervous; my heart was beating a mile a minute. And I was upset, and hurt, and angry. But I wasn't crying. Everything had suddenly become very clear in my mind and in my heart.

I knew that Tye was the guy for me; I was sure that Tye was the love of my life. We'd met through friends about two years earlier, when I'd first become a Dallas Cowboys Cheerleader, and we'd started dating about four months after that. Even though he couldn't commit to a dinner date, we hung out often. I saw him almost every night after cheerleading practice. He invited me to the *Entourage* party at his house every Sunday night, which usually included about a half dozen of his friends hanging out to watch the show. And I often met up with him and his buddies wherever they were hanging out; typically a bar or a restaurant.

My life was intertwined with his for a year. During that time, I'd done that thing that girls do: Fallen for him . . . even though he had not only NOT encouraged it, he had actively discouraged it. And I'd fallen harder than I had ever fallen before. As far as I was concerned, Tye and I had just completely clicked. Everyone always talks about a "spark," and we definitely had that. Plus, he was cute and funny, and he cared about building a career and starting a family, all of which made him seem like the perfect catch.

One of the main problems in my relationship with Tye was communication . . . we didn't really have any. Not about serious topics like our relationship, at least. I figured I knew him well enough to be clear that if I told him how I felt, I'd scare him off. So, I just never said anything. Because I'd been too afraid to tell him how I felt, I'd decided to show him. This meant going to Starbucks and leaving coffee and a muffin for him at his condo EVERY morning before work. And baking him cookies in the shapes of the teams that played the Dallas Cowboys, so he could eat them while he was watching the games on Sunday with his buddies. And picking up Chick-fil-A or pizza for him and the guys before away games, which I had off because the cheerleaders didn't travel with the team, and dropping off the food at his place. And sending him endless texts, and jokes, and emails, just to let him know I was thinking about him. (Oh gosh . . . I'm CRINGING right now, remembering how I used to behave . . . !)

Yes, I made sure that Tye knew that I liked him, all right.

The fact that none of this had caused him to want to be with me didn't discourage me. I was convinced that he was in love with me. He just didn't know it yet, not really. All I had to do was stick around until he realized his feelings for me . . . and I was willing to do that. But maybe he didn't *really* know how I felt. I mean, I had never told him. I had just assumed he knew because of all the ways I showed him. So . . . maybe . . . all I had to do was tell him how I felt.

While I sat on Tye's bed, waiting for him to come home, I passed the time by going over my ultimatum speech again, and again. It wasn't even an option in my mind that he might tell me that he didn't love me, and that he wanted to end the relationship. I really thought this "talk" would fix everything that was wrong with our relationship. He probably didn't know that I liked to be taken on dates (I mean . . . they are a little overrated), or wanted to be sent flowers, or sweet messages, or just told that I was appreciated, or loved even.

After waiting for about two hours, Tye finally got home and came into his bedroom. He was surprised to see me, but he didn't make a big deal out of it. He sat down next to me on the bed.

I took a deep breath. And, just like that, it all came spilling out of me. I was pretty heated at this point, just because I'd had two hours to stir up my feelings and make myself angrier.

"Listen, we've been dating a year, and I need to know where we're going," I said. "I feel like I put so much effort into you and into this relationship, and I feel like I get nothing back! I care about you. I care about you a lot. I love you!"

Now, we had never said the big "L" word before . . . heck, we'd never really said the "like" word before. And here I was, skating on very thin ice. But I couldn't help it.

It's how I feel . . . he needs to know!

He didn't say anything, not a single word. I think he was dumbfounded. Poor guy. I don't blame him. I think he thought my head was about to start spinning.

So, rational as I was, I kept talking. Well, it was actually more like yelling. There's nothing worse than not getting an answer of any kind, and the longer he stayed quiet, the angrier, and angrier, I became. I've never been a violent person, but I could have slapped him right then, just to get him to say something . . . anything. I wanted to do it, if only to shock him and get a rise out of him, but obviously, I didn't.

I doubled the force of my words and continued my tirade. Did I mention that I'm not the best communicator? Back then, I just might have been the WORST communicator. *This is how I thought a conversation about feelings should go!*

I think the reason that everything came out of me as anger was that I had been feeling all of this for so long, and wanting something from him so badly, and getting no response when I finally expressed my needs, it just pushed me over the edge.

"I need to know how you feel about me!" I said. "Because I don't know if I'm wasting my time. I know I'm only twenty-four, but I'm not the dating type, I'm the relationship type. If that's not what you want, you need to tell me now. I feel like I'm not high on your priority list at all! I feel like your work, your workouts, and your friends rank way higher on the list than I do! I do everything I can for you, try to make you happy, and I feel like you give me nothing!"

Sound familiar to any of you?

And that's just what I got from him right then, too: Nothing.

After all that I'd said, I got zero reaction from him. His silence just made me more heated and more irrational. Now, when I say Tye said nothing, I literally mean that he said nothing. I'm not sure why. Maybe he really was dumbfounded. This was a side of me that he had never seen before. How could he possibly know how to react? Maybe he was internalizing everything that I was saying, since he had never really heard me talk like this before. I did know, though, that his silence was not meant to be mean or to hurt me. Tye had repeatedly said throughout the course of our relationship that he just wasn't ready for me. Like so many other twenty-six-year-old males, he had a lot on his plate, and looking for a serious girlfriend was not his priority. I knew this.

But after dating for nearly a year, having so many amazing times together, where we laughed and had so much fun—meeting each other's families, meeting each other's friends (well, I met HIS friends, he couldn't be bothered to meet mine)—I needed to know where the relationship was going, how he felt about me, why I was never a priority, and what I could do to make him want to be with me.

I know, I know, it sounds like I wanted him to give me a PowerPoint presentation on why our relationship wasn't working, or something equally unlikely, but, really, I just wanted something from him; even the smallest explanation about what he was thinking—or, rather, *feeling*—about me. I wanted him to stand up for us, and if he couldn't, I wanted him to apologize for letting me down, and for letting US down. Or even just to hear him admit that he knew he took me for granted, and that he was sorry.

But, still, I got NOTHING.

Unbelievable.

His face was blank, and he remained silent. After all of that, I was so upset and desperate that none of what I said came out right, but I couldn't stop myself. It had been building for so long that when I finally unleashed my feelings on him, it was a massive attack. If only I had known how to fight, or if only he had felt inspired to even try.

"Fight for me, please!" I said. "Show me that you care about me at all! Say anything, because I'm leaving, and I'm walking out that door! I'm done with this relationship if you can't fight for me!"

Tye just sat there staring at me.

Seriously?? I think I've made a pretty good case. I even dropped the "L" word! And I'm getting NOTHING?!

By this point, I was crying . . . well, more like uncontrollably sobbing.

I stood up and stormed out of his room, down the hallway, and out the front door. To really make my point (as all rational women do), I slammed the door behind me as hard as I could. But I couldn't leave. I stood in the yard, pacing and crying and going over everything in my mind. Even though it hadn't gone like I'd wanted it to AT ALL (and it was beginning to dawn on me that maybe there wasn't anything I could say or do to make it right between Tye and me), I couldn't walk away. I loved him, and I knew I was losing him. There was also a small (okay, a large) part of me that really thought Tye would follow me out and chase me down so that I wouldn't have to leave like this.

But he didn't.

So . . . I yanked open the front door, rushed *back* into the hallway, and flew through the door into his room. He was still sitting there, staring blankly, like he didn't know what had just happened. I couldn't stop, so I started up right where I'd left off, telling him how much I loved him and all of the other feelings and dreams I had hidden from him for so many months, as well has how taken for granted I felt. I was still crying, so I talked as best as I could through the tears. Tye watched me warily, still not saying anything.

After a few more minutes of this one-sided conversation, I ran outside again. Making it a point to slam the door once again. And, again, I paced in front of Tye's condo. I couldn't bring myself to leave. It was beginning to sink in that once I left, our relationship would be over. I didn't want that. Even if I just had a little of him, it would be so much better than not having him at all. I couldn't stand the thought of losing Tye completely.

So . . . I swung around to go back into the house for a *third* time. But when I turned the knob, the door wouldn't budge. I shook it.

He'd locked the door on me!

I was beyond hysterical at this point, crying, desperate. Sure there was some right thing I could do or say if I just had the chance to keep explaining myself to this man who I loved so deeply.

Maybe if I could just apologize? I mean, this fight we were now having was all my fault, and I knew I was acting crazy and not like myself. But if I could just say the right words to make him *get it,* then it could all be okay again. I stood outside, banging on the door. I didn't care that it was two in the morning. I didn't care how I looked. My heart was broken. I couldn't give up and just walk away.

Finally, Tye opened the door. He stood in the doorway for a moment, looking defeated, before letting me back in.

I don't honestly remember most of the details about this point in the night, because I was so consumed with emotion. But I'm sure I wasn't making any sense at all. I'd gotten everything out that I needed to, and then I was just left in hysterics because I knew I was losing him. There was nothing I could do or say, so I was reduced to repeating, again and again, the only words that came into my head.

"I'm sorry, I'm sorry, I'm sorry," I said. "I shouldn't have said anything. I didn't really even mean it!"

As those words left me, I still had enough wits about me to know that it wasn't coming out the way I wanted or needed it to, and that I was beyond knowing what I was trying to get across anymore. But I still couldn't stop.

After my final rant, I took a deep breath.

It was over. I had nothing left to give. Nothing left to say.

I stormed out of Tye's condo one last time, slammed his front door, and walked out to my Honda Accord. Once in the driver's seat, I collapsed over the steering wheel and bawled. Actually, to say I bawled is an understatement. It was more like one of those complete emotional meltdowns that exhausted five-year-olds have. I was beyond reason or rationality.

But I still had hope.

Maybe he'll come after me. Maybe once he's had a chance to let my words sink in, he'll realize he had been wrong, and he will chase after me. I'm sure he's just letting things sink in right now . . . but he'll stop me before I leave for good.

I had finally stood up for myself, but I did it thinking that he would say, "Don't walk out. Don't leave."

And, instead, not only had he actually left the door wide open, he hadn't stopped me from walking through it. But I hadn't admitted that to myself yet. I still sat in the car and kept waiting for him to come and tell me that he'd made a mistake, that he'd fight for me, and that he was sorry he had made me sad.

So I sat there and waited.

Five minutes . . .

Ten minutes . . . Then, I saw Tye's bedroom light go off. My body was heaving and shaking, torn apart by grief. I couldn't catch even a single breath.

He's done. He has locked me out and is going to bed. How could he just let things end this way??

I couldn't breathe. I couldn't think straight. I couldn't grasp what had happened. Part of me was convinced that I should circle around the block and go back again; that there was still something that could be said or done to win him back. But I was finally beginning to accept what I knew inside: It was over.

So I headed home. Thankfully, I was living with one of the other Dallas Cowboys Cheerleaders in an apartment that was only about two minutes away (don't think that was any coincidence), so it wasn't a long drive, even if it was a miserable one. I kept asking myself again and again, *What did I just do? Why did I do that?*

It was two or three in the morning by this point, but it was a Friday night, and my roommate, Leah, was awake when I got home. I was glad to see her, but her boyfriend was over, and that just made me feel worse. Here I was, coming home by myself after the worst night of my life, and there she was, all cozy and happy with her boyfriend. They might as well have told me that they'd just gotten engaged.

I sat down on her bed. She sat down next to me and looked at me with concern, wondering what had just happened. Because to look at me, you would have thought somebody had just passed away.

"I think it's over," I said. "I think the relationship's over."

She went and got ice cream out of the freezer and tried to be a good friend. But I was not interested in ice cream or anything she had to say. I don't know what can be said to console somebody at that point anyhow. I'll be honest, she was talking, and all I remember was her mouth moving. I don't remember any of the words. It was like the schoolteacher in the *Charlie Brown* cartoons: *"Wah-wah-wah-wah-wah."* I was too busy replaying what had just happened with Tye.

Did I really just do that? Did I really just mess this up, and say this, and do that, and go back a million times, and look like a psycho girl, and yell at him, and slam the door behind me every time I left?

We sat there for I don't know how long, with me crying and her trying to console me.

And I mean, bless her heart, she just kept saying, "I don't know what I'm supposed to say."

Well, there was nothing she could say. There was no calming me down.

Finally, I realized how completely emotionally exhausted I was. I stood shakily, walked out of her room, crawled into my bed with my makeup and clothes on, and pulled the covers up as high as they would go. I was sure there was no way I was going to be able to fall asleep. But my eyes were burning from crying for so long, and I had hit that emotional wall where I just didn't have it in me to stay awake anymore. Before I knew it, I fell asleep.

●

I woke up in the morning, and my first thought was, *Did that really just happen? Did I really just do that? Maybe it was all just a bad dream, and none of it had actually happened.*

And then, I realized I was in the same clothes from the night before, and my eyes were all puffy and swollen from crying so hard, and I knew that the worst thing I could imagine had happened.

It's over. And it's my fault.

But then, I got up to my old tricks again. Guys would call it pathetic. Relationship books would call it unacceptable. I called it persistent.

I didn't really know if it was 100 percent over. I knew we'd had this huge fight, and I knew I'd said I was leaving, but neither of us had actually said that the relationship was over. No one had said: "Don't call me. Don't text me. I don't ever want to see you again."

So maybe it wasn't really over.

I lay in my bed forever, trying to figure out if we really broke up or if we had just had a really bad fight.

If only I hadn't done that last night, we'd still be together. We'd still be going out, and everything would be great. Even if I wasn't getting everything I wanted, I'd still rather have him in my life than have to live without him.

The whole time I was over at his house the night before, he had never said anything. And so, I had no idea what he was thinking, or feeling. And that made for a very odd end to the evening, and an even more confusing morning after, which led to a lot of wondering for me. But I was certain that, deep down, he was hurting just as badly as I was. That he didn't want to lose me anymore than I wanted to lose him. That he would surely call me to clear things up, and we'd be fine again.

I was sure I would hear from him. There was no way we could have a confrontation like that, without him wanting to clear it up.

But, then, reality set in.

Part of me thought he would call me to apologize, or to have his say, or to at least see if I was okay. And part of me knew that if he hadn't said anything yet, he probably didn't have anything to say.

So, rational as I was at this time, I called him. I'm sure that's breaking all kinds of dating rules. But I honestly didn't know what our situation was, and I couldn't stand the uncertainty.

He didn't pick up.

I left a voicemail. I had said I was leaving, but I still couldn't let go.

"I'm not sure what I'm supposed to say now, and I don't know if I'm even supposed to be calling you," I said in my message. "I'm sorry about what happened last night, but maybe we could just talk about it?"

And then, I hung up, and the waiting really began . . .

two

THE WAITING

was beyond heartbroken. I couldn't eat. I couldn't talk. It was a wonder I could even breathe. Yes, I was everyone's favorite girl to hang around with during this time.

That's why we have best friends: so we don't have to deal with moments like these by ourselves. The last thing I wanted was to be alone. I felt as if I was going stir crazy, and I just needed to do something, anything, to keep myself busy and occupied. (Well, at least physically, since emotionally, I was very much occupied.)

As soon as I hung up after leaving my message for Tye, I called my best girlfriends, Reagan and Stefani, who have known me since we were in college at the University of North Texas. I was soon in my car and on my way to see them. They were both happily married and living about thirty minutes outside of Dallas. Neither of them was a big fan of Tye, as he had never gotten serious enough about me in the year that we'd dated to ever bother meeting them. But they did their best to listen and be sympathetic.

At the end of the day, I couldn't stand the thought of going back to my apartment, so I stayed over at Stefani's house. Tye had helped me move into my place, and so I associated everything in it with him: the furniture he'd helped me put together; the happier days when he had been there with me; the fact that it was right around the corner from where he lived. Everything about it—even the smell—made me think of him.

To be completely and embarrassingly honest, in another classic psycho-girl move, a large reason that I chose to live in this particular apartment was because it was two minutes from Tye's condo. (I wouldn't have wanted the cookies I baked for him to get cold on the way over to his house, now would I?) And, of course, now that we were broken up, the proximity to him was agony.

I didn't want to see if his car was out front. I didn't want to see his car drive by. I really didn't want to see him driving by with anybody else in his car. If I had seen him with another girl, I think I would have literally cried my eyes out of my head. Even if it had been his buddies, I would have been wondering: *Where's he going? What's he doing? Are they going to meet up with other girls?*

I did frequent drive-bys (guilty as charged): *Is his bedroom light on? How many cars are parked out front?*

I hated doing all of this psycho-stalker stuff, because it really upset me. But be honest, ladies: Who hasn't done the infamous drive-by on an ex-boyfriend? I couldn't stop. I was acting like a madwoman! I felt consumed by this feeling of total emptiness. Anyone who's been through true heartbreak knows that feeling.

Now, keep in mind, at this point, Tye and I still had not had any communication. We hadn't talked, texted, emailed, or seen each other in weeks. I knew there was a huge risk of running into Tye and his friends out in Dallas, so I completely avoided the neighborhood.

I literally moved in with my married friends, Reagan and Stefani in the suburbs, and tried to find some sanity, which even I could see was severely lacking from my life at the time. When I wasn't at work, I was with the two of them, all day, every day, and I'd spend the night over at one of their houses. It got to the point where I stopped pretending that we were going to do something fun when we hung out, like we used to do. I would call on my way over and say, "I'm coming to sit on your couch." And I would. I would just sit there. Not talking, not eating, not smiling. (Well, that probably goes without saying.) I was miserable. I lost a lot of weight and looked like a hot mess. But there was nothing to be done for me. And I still could not be left alone, because I would drive myself crazy with my thoughts.

Reagan and her husband, Sean, were house hunting at the time, and some days, I would just sit in the back of their car while they went in and out of houses, because it was literally unbearable for me to be by myself.

Sean and Joe, Stefani's husband, were involved in a Denton County Fall Festival washers tournament. Washers is a game we play in Texas that involves trying to throw metal washers into a cup from a distance. I'd never been a fan of the sport, but at that point, even watching grown men throw things sounded better than being alone. And so I tagged along.

I honestly don't know what I would have done without my friends. They interrupted the ongoing dialogue in my head about how unloveable and stupid I was. They boosted my self-confidence. They said exactly what I needed them to say: "Melissa, you're so funny." "Melissa, you're so pretty." "Melissa, you've got so much going for you."

It was a nice effort, and greatly appreciated. Even though it was hard for me to believe all the kind stuff they were saying about me, it was exactly what I needed to hear to start building myself back up. The girls, of course, were my lifeline during this time. But Joe and Sean, who were like big brothers to me, did something that was almost more important: They gave me the guy perspective on my situation.

Both said the same thing: "I don't know what guy would treat you like that. We look at you as this fun, outgoing girl that loves life. You're independent. You've done some great things. Why would Tye treat you like this? Why wouldn't he want to come meet us when you were dating? You're better off without him."

When I heard this, it made me feel good, because I knew that most guys didn't line up to have this kind of heart-to-heart talk. So I felt like they really must have meant what they said if they were actually moved to speak up.

After a few weeks of being quiet and moping around, I got to the point where all I wanted to do was talk about my relationship with Tye. Our breakup consumed me. (As if *that* isn't obvious.) I had to analyze it to death, evaluating every last little thing that had happened between Tye and me over the past year, asking anyone who would listen: "Well, do you think we broke up because of this? Or that?"

I was desperate for answers or for someone to shine some light and hope my way. I'm sure I drove my friends nuts. But they never let on. Luckily for me, I couldn't have asked for better friends than Stefani and Reagan. They remained patient throughout it all, listening when I needed to talk and letting me be quiet when I was too sad to say anything.

My cheerleading friends were also great, but they wanted me to start dating again, no matter how much I said I absolutely was not ready. Soon after the breakup, they tried to introduce me to some random guy when we were out one night. I was as polite as I could be. But it made me realize that they didn't really get how I was feeling just then. I told them AGAIN that they weren't listening to me, and that I had no desire to date some guy. I know they didn't intend for me to jump into another relationship; they just wanted me to meet people and be social. I just didn't even have it in me to pretend to be interested when my heart still completely belonged to Tye.

Things were not only difficult in my personal life. I was also struggling in my professional life. I was working as a marketing rep for a liquor distribution company. Not necessarily my goal in life, but it paid the bills. I had been a finance and marketing major in college, because I had been told that the business world offered the most job opportunities. I'm not sure what I was expecting to do with my degree beyond that. I honestly think I was just looking for something to keep me afloat until I could find my true calling.

I remember the first day of work after my breakup with Tye. I actually called the receptionist for help before I went in that morning. She was about my age, and we were friends who shared confidences from time to time. I explained what had happened and asked her to do me a big favor before I could come into the office. I needed her to go into my cubicle and take down all things Tye. Pictures. Notes. Romantic quotes. Basically everything I had used to decorate my cube. I literally sat in my car in the parking lot while she threw away my mementos from the relationship.

Not that I was capable of doing much work once I finally dared to face my cube. All that week, I would be fine for a little while, and then, I would be consumed with how heartbroken I felt all over again. I remember thinking: *I am the most miserable I've been in my entire life, and there is nothing that can make me feel better.*

Almost every day at work, I would just randomly start crying. It would happen out of the blue, and there was no stopping my tears. I sat up front at the receptionist's desk and cried. I hid in the cube that belonged to one of my other work friends and cried. I sat on the floor in my cube, in my work clothes, with my boss sitting in a chair next to me, and cried. The crying didn't make me feel better. But I couldn't stop. When I finally did stop, even for a few minutes, it wasn't long before I was crying again. Now, I'm not usually an overemotional type of person, so this was very uncharacteristic of me. There's just something about that infinite feeling of hollowness following a breakup that produces far more tears than usual.

I had felt this way once before, when my relationship with Josh, my boyfriend in high school and college ended. But I think the intensity of those emotions was really a sign of immaturity on my part at that time. When you're with someone for so long, and you're so young, you don't quite know how to handle your emotions when it doesn't work out. But the difference was that I had gotten over my college heartbreak fairly quickly. I got sad, I got mad, I moved on. But with Tye, I got sad, I got mad, and I could not move on.

It didn't help that I was bored and frustrated with my mundane, routine job, which wasn't giving me any satisfaction. The people I worked with were great, but I'm just not someone who can sit at a desk for eight to nine hours a day, staring at a computer screen. I need to be up, doing things and talking to people. I constantly need new challenges to keep me interested, so I wasn't happy being so confined, and that job was not a good fit for me. As miserable as I was, I started looking for something—*anything*—that could make me feel better, or at least distract me from how badly I felt. Keep in mind, I *still* hadn't heard anything from Tye.

I was experiencing another professional low in my life at the time, because I'd decided to walk away from the Dallas Cowboys Cheerleaders. Back in February, just before Tye and I broke up, I had reached the end of my second year as a Dallas Cowboys Cheerleader, and it was time to decide if I was going to try out again for a third year. As fun as it was, it also meant that between my job and cheering, I was facing down these insane eighteen-hour days. During the week, I worked from eight to five, and then I practiced from six to eleven. Not much room for a social life in that schedule. I also felt like cheering was taking me away from what I really cared about—you guessed it: Tye, and the life I wanted to make with him.

When I had started with the Cowboys, I was on my own, and I could throw everything into cheering and the squad. But by the end of the 2007 football season, Tye was the new priority in my life. And so being a cheerleader wasn't quite as fun anymore. During practice, I found myself wishing I could be having dinner with Tye, or watching weekly TV shows, instead of sweating on a football field. I hated that I couldn't go out and do anything with Tye on the Saturday nights before games, because I had to get up and be at the stadium at seven a.m. the next day.

So when we had been asked to make our final decisions about whether we were coming back to the squad, I turned in my NO. It had been an easy decision to make at the time. I felt 100 percent sure that I was ready to go on to the next stage of my life, with the guy who I wanted to be with forever.

Two weeks later, Tye and I broke up. I didn't have the guy anymore. Or the Cowboys. Suddenly, all I had in my life was my day job. This was awful, because I needed something to keep me busy at night to distract me from all that I didn't have. So I tried to go back to the Cowboys. I went into the Cheerleaders' office and made my case. I spoke with the director and choreographer of the organization and told them that I'd made a mistake, and that I would love it if they would consider letting me come back for the next season. I knew this was a big deal because they're an organization with a philosophy along the lines of: "If you're not all in, we don't want you."

I honestly have no idea why, but they decided to let me come back. Maybe it was because I was a two-year veteran, and so they were invested enough in me to give me a second chance. Or maybe my humility impressed them. They were very intimidating women, and it took a lot for me to go to them and admit fault and ask for forgiveness. Even though they had let me return, I knew I was going to be on thin ice for a little bit, and I wasn't going to have any room to screw up.

Most of the girls on the team were supportive, especially those who had become my close friends. But, of course, everyone knew I was returning because my relationship with Tye was over. And not all of the girls were 100 percent receptive, which made it difficult for me. I was given the stipulation that I wasn't allowed to go on the photo shoot for the calendar that year.

Fair enough.

But a few of the girls were constantly reminding me of this. They'd say things like, "Why are you at practice tonight when you're not even going on the calendar shoot?"

I didn't really care about the shoot, but some of the girls took it as an opportunity to make me feel as if I wasn't really a part of the squad anymore. My self-esteem was already shot, and I didn't have it in me to deal with mean girls just then. Plus, my heart wasn't really in it. I had been ready to move on and to settle down with Tye, and that's what I still wanted, not the life of a single Dallas Cowboys Cheerleader, no matter how many perks it gave me. Although the pay was minimal, the other advantages were considerable. I was given etiquette classes, which taught me how to conduct myself in so many different circumstances. They also coached me on how to give an interview. Being a member of the Cowboys Cheerleaders meant that we were often asked to give interviews about the organization and the team. And they obviously wanted to make sure that we sounded intelligent and knowledgeable. Of course, I didn't know at the time just how useful this particular skill would later come to be. Plus, football is everything in Texas, and the Cowboys are the ultimate. For two years straight, I had the best seat at Texas Stadium, and I got to wear a uniform that many girls wanted very much to wear. We were minor celebrities in the city, and we could get into any club.

But I didn't really care about any of that anymore after Tye and I broke up. I think I was expecting the cheerleaders to patch a hole in my life, which I soon realized couldn't be filled by anything. I lasted about one week before I dropped out a second and final time.

And then began, what is still to this day, one of the lowest times of my life. I remember having this feeling that I had lost absolutely everything that was important to me. I had just lost the guy who I loved. I had just lost the Cowboys, which was an organization that had basically kept me sane and had been such a positive outlet for me for the past two years. And all that I had left was a job that didn't fulfill me.

Soon, I would be twenty-five. And I had nothing checked off my list; the "List" that every girl makes when she's about thirteen years old; the list that should, theoretically, be checked off by the deadline you assume. (Note to readers: I found out that twenty-five is wayyyy too young to cap off the list!) Here was mine at the time:

Great Job: No.
Great Guy: No.
Great House: Nope.
Anything fun to look forward to: Absolutely not.
Pity party for one: Yes, please.

What I wanted more than anything for my birthday was just to hear from Tye. Even just a one-word text would be a sign that he was thinking of me. I hadn't heard a peep from him since our big fight, which was agonizing. As two weeks of radio silence passed, I knew with even greater certainty that things were not looking good for us to get back together.

But I still couldn't let go. I felt like I was in limbo. And I couldn't stop reaching out to him. I would find myself at work, watching the seconds drag by, and before I could stop myself, I'd have my phone in my hand. I'd try to control myself, but I never could. The next thing I knew, I'd find myself texting him:

"Hi. Miss you."

"Hey. Can you call me?"

And this wasn't just every once in a while, either. Every day I would text him any little thing I could think of, just hoping to get an answer. Boy, I really should have read a book on what *not* to do when going through a breakup. But no matter how many texts I sent, I still got no response.

I couldn't give up. I had this idea in my mind that Tye was just as miserable as I was, but that he was just being stubborn. He didn't want to be the one to call me because it would make him seem weak.

And so I felt like I had to call him—not just for me but for both of us. When I did call, it always went straight to voicemail. Even with the many times I called and texted him in those weeks, I never heard anything back from him.

I had found out that the day after we'd broken up, which was a Saturday, he'd gone to Southlake. This is his hometown, and his parents and brother still live there. So, of course, being Queen of Denial, I reasoned that he went home because the only people who could make him feel better were members of his family. And he obviously was just as crushed as I was about the breakup.

This was great! This was exactly where I wanted him to be after we broke up: hanging out with his family. Not going out with the guys and meeting girls. And talking to girls. And flirting with girls. But then I learned that he'd gone to Southlake just to attend his nephew's Little League football game. So much for my theory. Even worse, I soon started hearing from girls in Tye's circle that he really *was* going out and meeting girls, and talking to girls, and flirting with girls. In other words, he was fine. I never asked for these status updates, mind you, and I don't know why the girls gave them to me. (Maybe just a case of girls being girls?) If they could have felt how big the knife was that went into my chest when I heard about Tye with another girl, they might have thought better of it.

Finally, it was the day I had dreaded: March 11, my twenty-fifth birthday. First thing when I woke up, I checked my phone, hoping for some word from Tye. Nothing.

I went to work. Checked my phone. Nothing.

All of my colleagues took me out to lunch to help try to cheer me up.

I checked my phone. Still. Nothing.

That night, five of my closest friends, including Reagan and
Stefani, took me out for a birthday celebration at a themed restaurant
called Medieval Times. For those of you who are not lucky enough
to have a Medieval Times in your neighborhood, it is literally dinner
in a tournament setting. You eat with your hands . . . You drink out
of a jar . . . You watch knights battle in the arena . . . And—oh yes—
there's actual jousting, folks. My friends knew it was corny, but that
was supposed to be part of the fun. They were hoping that if they
went completely silly and over-the-top, I'd forget my heartbreak.
They had planned in advance to have the knights give me all of the
attention, so the knights presented me with roses, and they crowned
me the "goddess of love and beauty." It was all very sweet, but the
whole thing made me feel even more pathetic—especially because
there were only about ten other people in the whole place, and so
the mood of the entire evening was kind of sad, and lame, and low
energy. I found myself just sitting there, despondently staring off
into space.

*This is what's happened to my life? Seriously? This is my twenty-fifth
birthday, and I'm sitting at Medieval Times with five people, and the
knights are giving me a sash? This cannot be real.*

But it was. Painfully real.

I commend my friends for trying, even in the midst of my misery.
I'm sure I wasn't exactly good company, and I certainly couldn't
have sat home alone, especially as the night wore on with no word
from Tye. I was distraught. And I'm sure I didn't do much of a job
of hiding it from them.

That birthday is kind of what triggered everything that happened
afterward, including *The Bachelor*. I took stock of my life that night.
I was now twenty-five. I had a job that I didn't really care for. I was
not even close to dating somebody who I'd be with for the rest of

my life. I didn't have anything in my life that was just for me that I loved. Out of everything on my personal checklist, I had nothing. I felt empty and lonely.

This reality was very hard for me to face. I was coming out of a time in my early twenties when I had had a lot of momentum, and I had thought things would continue to go like that, or get even better, as I got older. I never expected anything like this. At the ripe old age of twenty-five, everything was falling apart.

Before Tye, I had been in a seven-year relationship with my high school sweetheart, Josh. It ended with me getting—you guessed it—dumped, and, even worse, he had cheated on me. But the fact that we had been together that long had made me feel, for a time, like marriage was just an easy step away for me. We broke up just two weeks before our college graduation. And! Here's the kicker: He was engaged by the time graduation came around (yes . . . in a whopping two weeks). Talk about being devastated. I felt taken advantage of and betrayed. For the seven years before our breakup, I'd had my life planned out, with the person I'd thought I was going to be with . . . and then, it was all pulled out from under me.

After being in a relationship from the age of fifteen, I was totally unaware of how to be an "I." I had been a "we" for as long as I could remember. But at that point, something inside of me just took over, and I went on autopilot. I graduated college. I moved forty-five minutes away to Dallas, got my own apartment, and found a job. I even saved up enough money to buy my own car. And I did it all by myself. Looking back, I realize that I was being pretty darn independent for a twenty-two-year-old!

When I couldn't quite shake the low self-esteem I felt in the wake of my breakup from Josh, I had sought out something bigger than me, an adventure, to take my mind off the past and push me into an even better future. That's when I became a Dallas Cowboys Cheerleader. Because this was something that was a challenge for me, it made me feel as though I had the power to accomplish things and improve my situation in life. I had assumed this would be true forever.

And so, when I was younger, I had gone ahead and mapped it all out. By the time I was twenty-five, I was going to have a six-figure job. I was going to own my own house. I was going to be married and working on having kids. I was going to be so happy.

Instead I was sitting in Medieval Times wearing a cardboard crown and a fake satin sash, holding my wilting roses. Not quite the American Dream that I had imagined for myself.

Tye remained MIA on my birthday. Clearly, he didn't want to have anything to do with me, and as long as that was the case, I was determined not to see him and let him know how hurt I was by his absence. As much as a part of me really wanted to see him, I continued making sure to stay away from the places where I might run into him. But, it was impossible for me to cut him out of my life completely, as I had done when Josh broke my heart at the end of college, and I left him, my old friends, and the entire city of Denton, Texas, behind. It wasn't as easy with Tye. We lived five minutes apart, and Dallas was my home now. Our lives were so intertwined; it was hard to avoid him or his friends.

I had managed to avoid seeing Tye for almost a month after we broke up. And then, St. Patty's Day rolled around. Even though I knew he'd be out on the town with his friends, I figured there would be a million people out in the city that night, and there was no way I'd run into him. As usual, Dallas had closed its downtown streets for its annual parade, which I had gone to with a couple of my girlfriends.

My roommate, Leah, and I had cut the sleeves and midriffs off of our T-shirts, and made them into these little halter tops, which we tied in the back and wore with jeans. When I looked in the mirror before I went out that night, I was feeling pretty cute for the first time in ages, which made me feel better about the possibility of running into Tye. Seeing him was always in the forefront of my mind, when I knew there was a chance (even a slim one!) that we'd cross paths. And then, my mind games would run wild: *It's probably real easy for him, if he doesn't see me. I mean, he is a very "out of sight, out of mind" kind of guy. But if he runs into me, it will probably stir up all of those intense feelings he had for me and maybe even make him want me again.*

And that, of course, was still my secret hope.

After the parade was over, a bunch of us girls went to Primo's Bar & Grille to grab some food. Ironically, it was where Tye and I had originally met, a year and a half earlier. But, despite my secret desire to see him, I truly felt that there was no way he'd be there that night, given all of the bars in the city, and so I wasn't expecting a run-in.

Of course, as soon as my girlfriends and I arrived, I looked up, and there he was, standing at the bar, looking cute in his light green T-shirt, jeans, and cowboy boots (yes, I still remember exactly what he was wearing). I felt like someone had just sucker-punched me in the gut when I saw him. It was that feeling you get when your heart literally drops into your stomach. The usual inner debate started in my head: Do I go say hi to him? Do I not say hi to him? Do I pretend I didn't see him and wait for him to say hi to me?

And then, we had that moment of completely awkward eye contact from across the room. And, to make things even harder, he was talking to a girl: some cute little blonde. Okay, okay . . . she could have very well been an eighty-year-old granny with a hunchback, but I saw a *Playboy* model. What stupid mind games we all play! I sat there, frozen, wondering what I should do. I didn't want to look, but I couldn't help myself.

I felt like I had to do something, since I hadn't seen or heard from him in a month, and I was desperate to know how he was, and how he'd been feeling. I knew this was my one chance to talk to him. So, finally, I walked up to him. As I did, I could feel these big crocodile tears forming in my eyes. I fought them back, thinking, *Don't cry. Don't cry.*

"Hey, how's it going?" I asked.

But it felt awkward. The tears were so close to the surface, and I was trying so hard to keep them in.

"Hey, how've you been?" he asked, nonchalantly, as if I was his buddy. "You doing okay?"

I paused for a second before I answered, and a huge tear ran down my cheek. "No, I'm not okay," I said.

He reached out with both of his hands and stroked my arms, just trying to calm me down. Looked me right in the eyes and smiled at me.

"It's going to be okay," he said.

All of a sudden, I was comforted.

Oh my gosh, so he DOES miss me. And he's going to call me after tonight. And the relationship is going to work out after all. He clearly wouldn't tell me it would be okay, if it wouldn't be, right? He definitely wants us to get back together!

Oh, Melissa.

Now, when I look back, I realize that that wasn't what he was trying to get across at all. What he meant was: You'll be okay on your *own.*

I think he just didn't know what to say, and his way of dealing with the emotional hot mess in front of him was to say that it was going to be okay.

I attempted to smile back at him. We said an awkward good-bye. I walked away and sat down with my friends again, but I kept looking back at him. I couldn't help it. He went back to talking to the little blonde girl who had been standing next to him the whole time. Their conversation didn't look particularly romantic, but it still hurt to watch. I kept thinking: *I was just up there. I just talked to him, and now he's talking to HER.*

I have no idea who she was—she very well could have been his cousin, but just the SIGHT of him interacting with a female tore me up inside.

My friends and I ended up leaving Primo's before our food order arrived. I'd thought that I would be okay if I saw Tye and that I'd be able to hide my sadness. But I failed miserably on both counts. And I could no longer deny that Tye was handling the breakup just fine. All of the pain and doubt that I had believed he was feeling existed only in my mind.

Tye was out and about. He was talking to his friends. He was chatting up girls. Meanwhile, I was still totally miserable. And my heartbreak got worse when I had to admit that the reason that Tye hadn't been in touch was because he didn't miss me, and NOT because he just didn't know what to say. And then, I started analyzing everything all over again and feeling like maybe he had wanted to break up with me all along. And I had finally given him an out that night when I exploded on him. I had probably made it very easy for him to move on without even realizing it.

Yes, I was a complete mess.

At the same time, I still couldn't completely let go of him.

While I definitely wasn't stalking him, I looked for any excuse to have contact with him. I must have been a glutton for punishment. His birthday was in early April, and so I sent him a text wishing him a happy birthday. And then I waited. And waited. And waited.

three

·

BREAKUP
PURGATORY

About another month passed. I had survived not hearing from Tye. I had survived seeing Tye. I was just starting to get to the point where, although I wasn't feeling good, I could at least dress myself, comb my hair, and form complete sentences again. But I swear, it's like guys are born with some kind of radar, and they can sense just when they're starting to lose their hold on us and need to reel us back in.

And I felt the full force of that gravitational pull one evening when I was out with my good friend Robin. We were having a great girls' night out. We went to dinner and had lots of girl talk (that didn't include boys . . . well, not one *particular* boy, at least). And we went dancing. At one point in the night, we went into the bathroom together (as girls always do), and while we were primping, I got a text message.

Oh my gosh, it's from Tye!

It said: "I miss you."

Short. Sweet. To the point.

I literally collapsed on the floor in the bathroom. I was in complete shock. Robin laughed and took a picture to show me how dumb I looked, lying on the floor with my phone in my hand. We still laugh over that picture today.

But, back to the text message!

Okay, to be completely honest, this wasn't the FIRST time I had heard from Tye since we broke up. After I texted him to wish him a happy birthday, he had written me back. But all he had said was: "Thanks for remembering." Romantic, right?

Yeah buddy, that's not QUITE what I was hoping for, but you're welcome. I GUESS.

But this note was different. HE MISSED ME! And it was completely unprompted on my part! This was what I had been hoping and praying for! But to be honest, by this point (three months since the breakup), I was actually doing semi-okay. I wasn't completely consumed by my heartbreak anymore, and I had stopped expecting to hear from him.

Needless to say, I was beyond happy! Of course, after what Tye had put me through, I should have known better than to get sucked back in. But, immediately, I was a goner. AGAIN. I sent him a text back telling him that I missed him, too. And he wrote me back and asked me to stop by his house. How could I not?

He actually WANTS to see me? And HE'S initiating it? Of course I will!

So . . . I went over. It was the first time I'd seen him since St. Patty's Day. When I got to his house, we played music from his iPod and sang and danced with each other all night. It was as if we'd picked up right where we had left off. No awkwardness. No mention of a breakup. Just good old-fashioned fun. I left his house with a huge smile on my face. And that still remains one of the best nights that he and I have ever shared.

After that initial text from him, we were in contact pretty regularly. Tye knew I really wanted to see the first *Sex and the City* movie, which had just been released. He asked me if I wanted to go see it with him that Friday night. I knew we weren't together at this point, but CLEARLY this was HUGE progress!!

It was his idea.

He had actually planned a real date. IN ADVANCE.

We NEVER went on dates, even when we were together. This was a new development, and I immediately thought: *See, he DOES want me back. He totally missed me! He IS really trying. He is a good guy.*

Now, I had already seen the movie with my girlfriends, but, of course, I didn't tell him that. I did not want anything to get in the way of this date. And nothing was going to keep me from being happy while we were on it. I made sure to make a big deal about how excited I was and how much I appreciated everything he was doing.

Not that it was all perfect. While we were out that night, we saw one of the girls I had cheered with the year before. We went over to talk with her, and when I introduced her to Tye, I didn't know what to call him. I wanted to introduce him as my boyfriend, but I didn't want to scare him off. So I decided to play it cool. Cool and very casual.

"This is my friend Tye," I said.

Neither of them noticed that anything was out of the ordinary, and we got through the awkward moment. But, internally, I was overanalyzing the situation, wondering if Tye had noticed that I had just used the word *friend,* and if so, what he'd thought about it, if anything.

Other than that, it was just so great being with Tye again. We laughed and talked and did what we did best: pretended as if the last few months had never happened. He didn't want to bring it up, and I didn't want to bring it up, and so we avoided talking about anything emotional or real. Just like before, communication was a big problem for us. During that whole time, we lived our lives with so many important issues on the back burner. But, as we learned, back burner or front burner, it still burns.

Neither of us was ready to deal with anything even remotely serious or upsetting. So we acted as though everything was fine. We acted like a couple, even. Tye drove me home and kissed me good night. I was in heaven.

I made sure to let him know how happy I was, and that I really liked being out with him, and really appreciated that he had asked me out and taken me on this great date. In my heart, everything was falling back into place, and I believed we were going to get back together and be really happy. And we were happy.

For a day or two—maybe even a week.

We fell into a pattern. We would have a great first date, maybe even a second date, and then engage in a flurry of texts—some silly and pointless, and others that made me believe that things were going to be okay between us. For instance, one text that I received from him while I was at work made me think that we had a future. We had been flirting via email and text all day long. He was teasing me about how much dinner I had eaten the night before (I've always been a big eater). And then, BAM! I got a text that took me aback: "Can you imagine how much you're going to eat when you're pregnant?"

Well, it's no secret how a girl's mind works. As far as I was concerned, he was thinking about me being pregnant, which meant he was thinking about me being pregnant with his baby!! Right?!? I was beyond happy. I was ecstatic!

And then, after a few days of fun flirting, the texts from him always stopped . . . just like that. After a weekend of great dates, on Monday, I'd get nothing . . . again. My heart would break all over again. On Tuesday, I knew I wasn't going to hear from him. It was the same thing on Wednesday and Thursday. Time lengths varied, but it was always between a week and three weeks of silence from him.

Then I'd get a text—"What's going on?"—which would lead to another amazing date.

And so it went. I see the cycle now, but I was just living in the moment and hanging on to any little source of hope he gave me.

I quickly learned: *This is our reality. This is how we work. I don't have a boyfriend. He doesn't have a girlfriend. We just hang out sometimes.*

It wasn't at all what I wanted. But I never said anything about how frustrated I was for fear of running him off again. If I had been stronger at that time, I would have said, "Tye, you need to make up your mind. You either want to be with me, or you don't want to be with me, but you can't keep doing this push and pull. It's not fair."

The worst part was, not only did I not stand up for myself, but I also let him get my hopes up every time. Just when I got used to having him back in my life, he would disappear again. For the next six months, our relationship followed this destructive pattern, and I never stopped it or even tried to learn from it. That's not 100 percent true, actually. If I were to be completely honest with myself, I'd have to admit that, deep down, a part of me knew what was going on. But I lied to myself and pretended that I was just playing it cool, and that we were both fine with keeping it light. Right . . .

I just did not have it in me to walk away. At the same time, Tye wasn't making it easy, either, because he wouldn't let me go. He didn't want to give me the deep relationship I craved, but he clearly wasn't ready to lose me completely. Maybe he was keeping me at arm's length because he had a fear of commitment. Or maybe he was just that naïve about relationships and didn't realize what was required or what I deserved. Or maybe I was just that girl he called when he got bored. Who knows?

It may have just been more denial on my part, but I became convinced that he would come back eventually and want me to be his girlfriend again. I just knew, somehow, that he wasn't going to find somebody else and leave me for good. But I also started to understand that, in the times when we weren't seeing each other, I was free to do whatever I wanted, just like I guessed he was doing at the time.

It took a while, but that realization finally gave me a little bit of the independence I hadn't had before. And, honestly, every time we'd get back together and then not talk again, it did make me slightly stronger. I was regaining some of my power, but it definitely came in baby steps. I was still very much in love with Tye, and so dating anyone else was out of the question. But I was at least functioning on my own during the times when we were not talking. I went out with my friends. I was slowly getting my life back together.

But I definitely broke one of the *Cardinal Rules of Girlfriends.* If I had plans with my friends on a Saturday night, and Tye just happened to call me out of the blue, I immediately dumped my friends and went out with him. I know, I know: That's like Rule Number One. But I couldn't help myself.

Finally, my friends had had enough. "Why do you let him do that?" they asked.

I always had an excuse, and I always defended him.

"Well, you know, he's young," I said. "He doesn't mean to hurt me. I don't even think he knows he's hurting me; he's just very wrapped up in what's going on in his life right now. He's only twenty-seven and not really ready to settle down . . . yet."

Of course, this argument didn't fly with Reagan or Stefani. Both their husbands were twenty-five—younger than Tye—and these guys not only were married but were *happy* to be married. Well, that blew my theory.

I had to admit to myself that guys who weren't afraid of commitment and who wanted to settle down did exist. It wasn't even that I wanted to be married right then, but I did want to be in a committed relationship, and I wanted the person who *I* wanted to be with to want to be with *me*. But, for right now, I was caught in a cycle. A bad cycle. And it didn't show any sign of getting much better anytime soon. I was in breakup purgatory.

I might not have been done with Tye yet, but my friends were. In a big way. They had seen me crying for the three months that Tye and I were apart, and they had seen me upset during the last few months when he kept coming in and out of my life. It also didn't help matters that they didn't even really know Tye, because he had never taken the time to meet them when we were dating. Maybe if he had, it would have been different. But as it was, although I was constantly saying what a great guy Tye was, they sure didn't see it. They didn't trust him. They didn't like him. They didn't want us to get back together again, because they were convinced I could do MUCH better.

They finally tried to do something about it.

That summer, we spent a lot of time out on Lake Dallas. My friend Stefani would always invite this guy along for me. So every weekend, it would be Stefani and Joe, Reagan and Sean, and then me and this random guy from Stefani's church. Talk about awkward! He was attractive. He was great. I wanted to like him. I really did. But my heart just wasn't in it. I knew I had already met the guy I wanted to be with. He just didn't want to be with me as much as I wanted to be with him.

They were good friends, though, and they were determined and willing to try anything to make me happy. They just wanted to see me smile again. More than once, when I was out to dinner with the four of them, and our waiter happened to be young and attractive, Stefani or Reagan would egg him on.

"Don't you think she's pretty?" they'd ask him, pointing at me.

Oh my gosh!! Mortified!

On the one hand, I was sitting there feeling totally embarrassed and pathetic. On the other hand, their positive reinforcement gave me the kind of attention I needed right then; that little something from a guy that said maybe I was worth wanting. My self-esteem was so low that it really helped to realize that if a guy could think I was pretty in a tank top with my hair in a ponytail, then maybe there was still hope for me. My friends might have been trying to embarrass me into another relationship; maybe they figured if they humiliated me enough, I'd give up and give in. But I guess I proved to be too stubborn for that strategy!

Despite the machinations of my friends, I didn't go on even one date that whole summer. I was still caught up in Tye, and I've always HATED dating. The idea of dating had never seemed fun to me, even when I wasn't a complete emotional wreck. I could never stand how awkward first dates were. And now, all I did was compare all other guys to Tye. In my mind and heart, Tye had everything that I wanted in a partner and no one else could measure up. He talked about his nephews and niece all the time, so I knew he was family oriented. He had always wanted to open his own insurance agency, and was doing all he could to make that happen, so I knew he was ambitious. He was funny and always made me laugh. He was a lot of fun to be around because he didn't take things too seriously (me being one of those things, unfortunately), and we always had a great time together. And of course I thought he was gorgeous—that helped!

Stefani and Reagan knew me well enough to understand that they shouldn't push me too hard to date other guys. But they were getting fed up with me. The two of them would roll their eyes whenever I talked about whatever latest thing Tye had done, bad or good. Just hearing his name was enough to make them crazy.

One day I was over at Stefani's house, and she finally snapped.

"I don't want to hear about it anymore," she said. "I'm your best friend, and I'm here for you, but if you're going to keep doing this to yourself, you can't keep running to me when he breaks your heart again. Because we do this every week."

I couldn't blame her for reacting that way. I understood why she and Reagan were tired of listening to me whine and moan. Heck, *I* was tired of whining and moaning. Despite Stefani's words, I knew that she'd still be there to pick up my pieces and listen to me cry when I needed her to, because that's what great friends do. But the whole situation had become almost as emotionally draining for her as it was for me.

And then, I got frustrated, too. It dawned on me that, sometime during the breakup, I had not only lost my motivation to meet someone else, I had also lost my motivation in pretty much every other area of my life. I didn't know if it was because I wasn't challenged by my job, and I didn't have any extracurricular activities I was passionate about, or whether it was because my personal life was a complete mess. I just knew that I felt completely paralyzed.

I was at a crossroads emotionally, and my life was at a standstill.

I constantly thought about how empty and hollow I felt. All I did, all day, every day, was sit and think about my failed relationship, and how—IN ONE DAY—my cube had gone from having happy pictures of Tye and me all over it, to having no decorations at all. It was like a metaphor for my life. I was stuck in this dark, empty space, and I didn't know how to get out.

I had that empty pit in my gut, and I just wanted it to go away, and Tye was just ONE factor that contributed to that pit (albeit, a big factor). I was not happy with where my career was. I was not happy having a home I didn't like going home to (because it reminded me of Tye). I was not happy that I didn't have the Cowboys to keep me occupied, and most of my friends were still on the squad. And I was not happy being alone. Even though I was with my friends all of the time at this point, ironically, I felt more alone than I ever had. So I just wanted a change from everything. Not limited to—but definitely including—Tye.

I needed a BIG change: a change of scenery, a change of perspective, a change of direction in my life. I was itching to get out of Dodge. I didn't want to be in Dallas anymore. I was thinking about relocating to Austin, and I visited there several times while contemplating whether or not the move would make me happy. I was thinking about going for my teacher's certificate and becoming a teacher, and I still believe I will be a teacher someday. But I couldn't bring myself to do anything.

And then, one day that summer, I checked my mail, and there was an application for the television dating show, *The Bachelor.* I was totally dumfounded. The opening letter read: "Thank you for applying to be a candidate on *The Bachelor . . .*"

What?? I never applied to be on anything. I wouldn't even know how to go about doing that if I wanted to. What the heck?

Now, over the past six months, several of my girlfriends had joked that I should be on that popular television dating show *The Bachelorette*. They always told me that I had a lot of things going for me, and that I would absolutely get picked for the show. But I thought it was just my friends trying to cheer me up and make me feel better about myself. I certainly hadn't taken them seriously. And I certainly hadn't applied to be on any show.

I couldn't figure out how the application came to me, but I also knew that it couldn't have been completely random. It wasn't like they just handed them out to people at the supermarket. The materials revealed no clues. They thanked me for my interest in becoming a contestant, and included instructions that asked me to complete the entire questionnaire as honestly as possible and mail it back by a certain deadline.

Hmmm . . .

I took the application to work the next day, sat with one of my colleagues who was also a good friend, and got my cell phone out. One by one, I called each of my friends and asked them if they had somehow nominated me to be on *The Bachelor*. Finally, I got one of my girlfriends from the Cowboys, Kristen, on the phone, and her response wasn't quite like anyone else's.

"You know, I might have," she said. "I don't remember."

Seriously?! You don't remember if you signed me up to be a contestant on a national television show? Yeah, right. Someone's busted. I found my culprit!

After that mystery was solved, I decided to delve further into the "application." As I've probably established by this point, I would have done pretty much anything to make my workday go by quicker. As I started flipping through the application materials, I noticed there were twenty-four pages of questions, all targeted at me.

Wow. They could write a biography on someone with all of the information they wanted.

I figured it wouldn't hurt to fill it out, since I wasn't exactly doing anything with my life just then. Surely I wouldn't make it. I'd just see how far I could go, just for fun. It gave me something new to focus on—a distraction—which I desperately needed in my life at that time. It certainly wasn't anything I had a burning desire to do. To be totally honest, I had barely even seen the show. And I had always thought it was a little staged.

Falling in love on TV? Really? With all those cameras?

I just didn't buy it.

Anyhow, I filled out the questionnaire. The questions were pretty basic:

Where are you from?
Who are your friends?
What do you like to do?

And, of course, they wanted to know all about my romantic life. When I got to the questions about my love life and past relationships, I decided to leave out Tye. I suppose it was probably just another form of denial.

If I leave it off the application, no one will ever know what really happened . . .

I filled it all out and sent everything back in, along with a couple of photos, which were required. I wasn't sure how long the whole process would take, since there wasn't a time line included in the packet. So after I mailed the application, I kind of forgot all about it and continued on with my life.

A few weeks later, I received another envelope in the mail from

The Bachelor. I'd made it to the next round. How, I have absolutely no idea. Next up was to submit a video of myself answering a whole slew of new questions.

I almost stopped right there. It was too much work. I didn't have a video camera. And I didn't really care enough to deal with all of this. Kristen and I were about to leave on a big, fun trip we had planned to Mexico with a couple of friends, even though I was completely broke at the time—emotionally and financially.

I had filled Kristen in on what was happening throughout the audition process and had kept her updated on each new round that I had made it through. I told her about the video, and how I didn't really want to do it. I was a little embarrassed and not really sure I was 100 percent interested. She somehow convinced me to just do it.

We literally shot the video the morning we left for Mexico. And we had to go to my parents' house to use their video camera. I laugh today when I see clips of that video on YouTube, because it's so clear that I was already dressed for a Mexican vacation! It's a terrible interview, really, because we were in such a rush, and I wasn't that invested in the whole process. The only thing I remember saying was in answer to a question about how my relationships tended to end.

That was easy.

"I'm always the dumpee," I said. "And I don't understand why. I believe in love. I've got a tattoo on my back that says True Love, because I'm a firm believer. I just haven't found it."

I shipped off the video, left for Mexico, and didn't think twice about it. Surely they wouldn't be interested in the quick, sloppy interview I'd submitted. It was fun to play the "what if?" game, but I was still planning to move on with my life, as if there was no possibility that anything would happen with the show.

Until, that is, the producers contacted me to say that they wanted to meet me in person.

What?!? How did I actually make it to the next round?

Again, I couldn't understand how, or why, they still wanted to meet with me. Looking back, maybe they saw how cracked and fragile I was at the time—even though I'd tried my best to mask my heartbreak. I suppose I'll never know for sure.

It was now Labor Day weekend. I was vacationing with my family on an island off the coast of Florida. It was a Rycroft family tradition; we'd gone there every summer for the past twenty-four years. I remember this trip being particularly uncomfortable for me. My younger brother, Christopher, had brought along his girlfriend, which was great, except that there I was, single and auditioning for a TV dating show, which my parents had made clear they really didn't want me to do. Not exactly the impression I wanted to make as an older sibling.

There were only two days I could choose to fly to Los Angeles for the audition, and so I had to leave vacation a few days early to meet with the producers.

I wasn't nervous or anxious at all. I never thought I would make it, and so the whole experience just seemed beyond belief. Once I got to LA, there was a car waiting to take me to the hotel where we were meeting. Once we arrived there, a producer was outside waiting to greet me. She seemed nice enough.

Maybe this won't be so bad after all.

She showed me to my room to drop off my bag, then escorted me immediately to where all the producers were set up.

First I did a one-on-one interview with a producer. She asked me a few generic questions that I'm sure everyone's been asked at one time or another, and I simply answered them the best I could.

So I answered, smiled, and had fun with the process. I didn't answer anything too seriously—I wanted to be funny and show that I had a sense of humor.

After the one-on-one interview, I was led into a room where—without any warning—I was suddenly face-to-face with a slew of producers, who were all sitting around a table staring at me. They made me sit up front and face them all.

Intimidate much?!

The strange thing was that I still wasn't the least bit nervous. While I was sitting there, I had this thought that made me feel totally calm: *They can't ask me a question I don't know the answer to because it's all about me.*

I also thought of it as a charade to see if I could cover up how I was really feeling, which was still about as heartbroken as I'd ever been. I never cried on camera. I never said anything directly about my relationship with Tye. I was acting like this really strong, independent woman. And it worked. (Well, I think it did. But, then, for all I know, they might have been on to me the whole time.) Even though I was still a mess inside, there was something about pretending to be put together that started to make me feel like I *was* that powerful woman I wanted to be, and that made it all easier.

It helped, too, that, somehow, I immediately had a good sense of my boundaries. They knew that I had been a professional cheerleader, and one of the producers tried very hard to get me to do a cheer.

I can't be THAT girl. If I dance and cheer now, they'll expect me to dance and cheer on the TV show . . . and that's just not me.

I smiled to make sure I didn't seem rude.

"I don't really cheer," I said. "I mean, the cheerleaders are dancers anyhow. They're not cheerleaders."

"Well, then, do a dance," the producer said. "We want to see a dance."

I could tell that they wanted to see how far I'd go on TV.

"No," I said firmly. "I'd rather not. I'm not really comfortable doing that. And I'm not dressed appropriately."

There was their answer to how far I would go: not far at all.

When I left, I figured I had totally blown it, because I didn't do what they wanted me to do. They probably wanted me to be that girl who would be THE DANCER on the show. But I didn't care. I was glad that I hadn't compromised myself. (How ironic that it actually took me doing a television show that I didn't really care about to inspire me to stand up for myself, and launch a change in my life that played a big role in my destiny.)

About a week later, I got another package from *The Bachelor* in the mail.

No way! . . . This has got to be a rejection letter or something . . . It can't be ANOTHER round of auditions.

I opened the package, and what do you know? It was a formal acceptance letter to be on the show! They wanted me to be a cast member! All I had to do was sign the enclosed contract by a certain date, and it would be official.

At first, I still couldn't believe I'd made it, even after this whole, long process I'd been through. Then, the reality of it all set in, and I realized that there was one huge obstacle I had to face before I could go on the show:

Tye.

Of course, I received the packet containing the contract just as

Tye and I were starting to talk again, and it felt like things were good between us. Naturally, it was hard not to get my hopes up. But, by now, I knew better. I gave myself a good talking to: "Melissa, remember the pattern. Remember that this happens for a week or two, and then he always goes away."

four

I THINK IT'S TIME FOR YOU TO GO NOW

didn't know what to say to Tye about *The Bachelor,* and so I chose not to tell him anything and just pretend like it wasn't happening. Part of me wanted to get out of Dallas, to go have an adventure, and leave my heartbreak and emptiness behind. But the other part wanted to stay and be with Tye, and not do anything that might upset our reunion. I couldn't muster up the courage to discuss it with him, and so I held on to the contract for as long as possible while weighing my options.

At the time, Tye was not the only factor I was considering.

Tye was just Factor #1.

Factor #2: I also had a full-time job. Factor #3: I had an apartment with my roommate, Leah, with whom I shared rent and bills.

I couldn't afford to go on the show and come back to no job. I wouldn't be able to pay rent on our apartment if I didn't have a job. And I certainly couldn't just abandon Leah.

Of course, Factor #1, Tye, was at the forefront of my mind. I wondered if there would even be a Tye to come home to afterward, if I went and did the show. Or maybe this would be the thing that would finally make him move on completely. As much as I still loved him, after months of being yanked around, I wondered if I even wanted him to be there when I got back. So there were a lot of issues that had to be dealt with, and I didn't even know where to start.

First, I decided I should deal with my job situation. It would be a make-or-break issue, since going on the show wouldn't even be an option, if they were going to fire me. I sat down with my boss and told him that I needed to take a leave from work. Because of the confidentiality agreement I had already signed for the show, I couldn't tell anyone where I was going or what I was doing. Try explaining that to your boss:

"So, I need to take some time off work," I said. "I can't really tell you why, or how long I might be gone. It could be anywhere from two weeks to three months. Will you hold my job for me, please??"

I know, I know, it sounded unbelievable to me, even as the words were coming out of my mouth. And it sounds just as ludicrous to me now. But, for some reason, he went for it. He said he could hold my job for me until I got back—I would just have to take an unpaid leave of absence.

Wow . . . Really?? That seemed too easy.

I could live with that; as we all know, I wasn't exactly in love with my job. And at least that was one major issue checked off my list.

Next up: The roommate. I sat down with Leah one night when we were both home. I really liked her, and I didn't want to make her feel like I was leaving her in the lurch. But I knew I had to explain what was going on and see what she said. I told her I was probably going to need to move out, but I wanted her to know that I would definitely stay if it were going to be a huge inconvenience to find a new roommate.

Shockingly, she totally understood, which was such a relief! She even had an idea for a replacement roommate—one of our fellow Cowboys Cheerleaders. We immediately called this girl to see if she'd be interested, and she said yes right then.

Fantastic!! Gosh, that was really easy, too!

I was so happy to have it work out.

Last up (and most important): Tye. This was the conversation I had been dreading the most because I really had no idea how he would respond. I felt that, in a perfect world, I could go have this great experience on *The Bachelor*. And then, I could come back home, and he'd still be interested in dating me. The worst-case scenario was that he'd get mad at me and never want to talk to me again. Of course, that would have devastated me. But, at least, that would have been something different to finally get us out of our rut. After six months of emotional turmoil, I was sick of not getting what I wanted, and not seeing any end to our pattern in sight. I was hoping that this wasn't going to be the end of us. But, either way, I had to do something.

I had had the contract for about two weeks, and I was facing the deadline for turning it in when I went over to Tye's condo for dinner. This was during one of our on-again times, which made it even more difficult for me to start this conversation I dreaded.

He picked up some sushi—which I loved! He knew sushi was my favorite food. This was just the kind of consideration I had wanted him to show me for the past year.

We sat up on the rooftop patio at his condo, which was one of my favorite places in the world to be. We had the radio turned on, and we were sitting there together, eating our sushi, talking and joking around, like we always did. Except, this night was different. I knew I needed to tell him that I was seriously thinking about doing *The Bachelor,* and that I might be leaving soon, but I didn't know how to do it. I had a pit in my stomach, and I'm sure I seemed nervous. I hated to bring anything like this up when things were so good . . .

What if I don't say anything, and we just continue like this, and then we're just good from here on out?

Oh, Melissa.

I still wanted things to work out with Tye so badly that I was eager to turn every good moment we had into proof that he wanted to be with me in the same way.

I was just working up my nerve to finally say something, when Tye handed me a manila envelope. I had no idea what it was, and I'm sure I had a confused look on my face as I took it from him.

"I want to talk to you," he said.

"Oh, okay," I said.

I looked at the envelope. My heart immediately started pounding in my chest. *What is this all about? I can't handle anymore surprises.*

"Open it," he said.

Inside was a chain of emails he had printed out. I saw that it started with an email from my friend Reagan to Tye, and then his email back to her. As I read, tears came into my eyes. I had no idea Reagan had done this, and her words were hard to face:

"Please leave her alone. She has such great opportunities now. She's going on *The Bachelor.* And she doesn't need you getting in the way and messing it up. Because she will give it up for you. If you care anything about her, or ever did, you need to let her go."

I read her words, and my hands started shaking. I couldn't decide if I was angry, or grateful, she had done this. It depended on

Tye's response. So I continued through the chain and read his reply
back to her:

"I promise you that I will support her and be honest with her. But
I will not promise to 'let her go.' I am sorry if this sounds 'selfish,'
but I am not going to ignore her if she calls and wants my opinion.
If she wants to go, I will surely not stop her."

Oh my gosh, he knows about this!

I was shocked. Shocked that Reagan had contacted him. Shocked
that he had written her back. Shocked that he knew about my secret.

I looked up to see the reaction on his face, but he was looking
down. His hands were on his head. I couldn't read him at all . . . I
didn't even know what my reaction was. But I did want to know
what he was thinking.

Was he okay with it? Was he upset?

Not that he really had any right to have a reaction, or to be
upset. He wasn't my boyfriend. He wasn't even really dating me.
If he was, he wasn't treating me with much respect. The email had
also contained a long explanation from him of why he felt like he
couldn't be with me, even though it killed him that he might risk
losing me because of it. He also mentioned our poor communication
and the problems it caused. I reread the line about where he was at
in his life and with our relationship:

> It kills me everyday to know that we are not together,
> and that in this "process" I may lose her. But the timing
> is not right. There are a lot of things going on in my life
> right now that I am unsure about (current job, starting
> a company, where I am living, *faith,* etc.), and until I get
> myself figured out, I can't afford to bring the person I
> care about most into my confusion.

It was so hard for me to read because he'd made it clear how much he cared about me after all, but he'd also confirmed that he wasn't able to get back together with me right now. This was definitely something that I needed to see. Parts of what he said made me feel good, but it also made my heart ache. Again.

Then I looked at the date on the email. He had received it more than a week ago and hadn't said anything to me about it. That absolutely crushed me. I stopped reading and looked at him until he finally looked up at me. Both of us sat there in silence for what seemed like forever. Then he told me that he had actually found out about *The Bachelor* BEFORE he got Reagan's email!

"My mom is the one who told me," he said.

Now I was really shocked. He had heard from his mom, of all people? Well, yes, because her best friend's neighbor was my best friend's mom, and she'd heard it from her. Now I was really embarrassed . . .

I didn't want his parents to know anything about this!

"Are you going?" he asked.

"Well, yeah, I think I'm going to go," I said.

I was still worried about his reaction, so I quickly tried to soften the blow.

"I'm not going to find a relationship," I said. "I'm not going to find love. Or be on TV. I just need something new. I need to get out of this rut that I'm in. I need a change in my life. I think I need to go."

He told me that one of his brother's ex-girlfriends had gone on *The Bachelor* about four years earlier, and she said she felt like she'd embarrassed herself.

"I won't do that," I said. "I'm really just going to go, you know?"

I suddenly felt so relieved that he already knew. I was still watching him closely, but it didn't seem to bother him! It never crossed my mind why it didn't bother him. I just assumed he was cool with letting me go grab a great experience, and then come home and start over with him. Of course, looking back, it makes sense that he didn't care, because he wasn't really emotionally invested in me right then. But in the moment, I was just happy that things were fine between us. The conversation ended, we went downstairs, watched TV, and acted (like we always did) like this huge conversation had never happened.

I was actually feeling pretty good, because it seemed like the best-case scenario to me: I got to go do this crazy, exciting new thing, and then, when I came home to him, he would probably still want to date me.

But I couldn't quite let it go. I wanted to beg him to give me a reason to stay, but I was still afraid of scaring him off. At the end of the night, when it was time for me to leave, I told him that there was still another option.

"I haven't signed my contract yet," I said. "It's not official that I have to leave. I don't have to go if you feel weird about it. I don't want to make you uncomfortable about anything."

I don't know where that came from, because now that I knew he wasn't going to fight for me to stay with him, I actually wanted to go. I was so disappointed that he couldn't be with me right then that I had quickly forgotten all of the caring things he had written about me in his email. I was hurt and mad and let down all over again, and I wanted to get away from him. But I still couldn't quite get clear of him. Whenever we were together, my feelings for him always rose to the surface and kept me from thinking clearly about what I really wanted, except for how much I wanted him.

And then, he spoke words that stabbed me straight in the heart:

"I think you should go. You should go and have fun."

WHAT???

I stared at him in shock.

Did he really just say that? Did he really not care if I left or not? Did he not realize that I was telling him I was going to go DATE someone else?!?

And then, even though it was the answer that I had wanted, anger came over me again, like the anger I had felt the night I waited in his room for him to get home so that I could finally confess my feelings for him. I shook my head in disbelief and walked out of his house. I was very calm. But, more important, I was now 100 percent sure of my decision. I was going to go. And I was absolutely going to make the most of my experience. I was fed up with trying to salvage a relationship that felt so one-sided. And for the first time, heartbreak or no heartbreak, I was genuinely excited about leaving and starting this new adventure in my life.

That next day, while I was sitting in my cubicle at work, I confidently signed my contract and mailed it off. A week later, I received confirmation that I was officially a cast member of *The Bachelor* Season 13.

Meanwhile, it had been announced that the new Bachelor was going to be Jason Mesnik, who had previously appeared on *The Bachelorette*. Now, I wasn't supposed to tell anyone that I was a contestant on the show, but of course, my best friends knew. They had been involved in the entire audition process. And as soon as they found out who the Bachelor was, "Operation Melissa & Jason" was in full effect. As far as they were concerned, anyone was better for me than Tye, and this guy actually seemed like he might be a catch.

One day, we were over at Stefani's house, hanging out and

trying to find something to do, when Reagan got a very devious look on her face and pulled Stefani and me into her office. We all crowded around the computer, and she started searching for videos of Jason on YouTube. Honestly, the Bachelor could have been an eighty-year-old man with no teeth, and they still would have found ways to get me psyched about him. At this point, although I was excited about going on the show, I was also determined not to fall in love with the Bachelor—no matter how wonderful he may be.

Reagan and Stefani pulled up video clip after video clip. They "oohed" and "aahed" their way through every single one. I couldn't help but smile. They were trying so hard to get me excited about going—and not just about going—but about dating, and finding a potential husband while I was there.

"Look how sweet he is," Stefani said.

"Look how cute he is," Reagan said.

"You could really, really be good with him," they both said.

Yeah, he lives two thousand miles away from me, he's seven years older than me (which wouldn't have really mattered, if I weren't being picky), and he's a contestant on a reality TV show. Sounds like a great fit . . . um . . . not really.

I was going through the motions because I knew my friends had been so good to me for so long, and they had a right to want me to move on and finally be happy. And, slowly, their efforts started to pay off. Maybe I was just fooling myself, but I did start to think: *He is cute. He is really sweet.*

And soon, I wasn't just pretending for my friends.

I felt like I had to be enthusiastic of my own volition, or at least try, because this was a way to FINALLY shake myself free from my cycle with Tye. I made a conscious decision to see *The Bachelor* experience as a fun adventure. If nothing else, I'd get to live in a mansion and not have to work for at least two weeks!

Stefani and Reagan may have been gung ho about me leaving to be on the show, but my parents were most definitely not. Every time I made it to the next round of *The Bachelor* auditions, I let my mom know. But she never really said anything. Her silent disapproval was really hard for me. Looking back, I think I really needed her support because I was in such a vulnerable place after Tye. Even more than that, I needed her approval and her encouragement, as I finally did something for myself—something that would force me to be independent again.

The fact that my mom didn't understand my decision made me doubt that my dad would, too. And so, I never brought it up in conversation with him. I imagined it would have been too awkward saying: "Hey, Dad, I'm going on TV to date one man along with several other women!"

My confirmation that my parents' feelings about my new adventure were less than enthusiastic came right after I had received my final contract from *The Bachelor*. I went over to their house for dinner, and I was completely dreading the conversation I planned to have with them. As we all know, it's the worst feeling to inspire disappointment in our parents. And I was well aware that I was at risk of causing them to experience it. Without too much small talk, I decided to just go for it—the whole ripping off the Band-Aid approach.

"So, I made it onto *The Bachelor*," I said. "And I think I'm going to do it."

My mom had no response at all, which is the one reaction that I absolutely can't bear. Nothing makes me crazier than silence, just like when I told Tye I loved him, and he didn't say a word. I stopped what I was doing and confronted her.

"Please understand why I'm going," I said.

"I don't understand it," she said. "I don't see why you have to leave town to date someone on a television show."

I immediately knew that not only was she totally against it, but nothing I could say or do would change her mind. I guessed that she and my dad had already shared confidences about it—how against it they were, how afraid they were that I'd do something to embarrass them, how they just didn't understand. Sadly, after that, it became something we didn't really talk about.

As I agonized over my final decision about whether I should go, I didn't share any of my thoughts or fears with my mother. When I finally chose to go, I told her the date I was leaving. And that was the end of the discussion.

Next up was tackling the logistics of the move. Preparing to leave for taping proved to be almost as big a feat as deciding to go! According to the producers' instructions, I had to pack for up to two months and be prepared for all types of weather, while keeping in mind the rules of looking good on TV: no white, no stripes, and no heavy patterns. But I was not told where I would be living or what life would be like, so I had no idea if I should pack for LA or for Alaska. It was hard enough packing for two months, let alone the fact that I didn't know where I was going, or what I would be doing when I got there. Included in the packet was a full-page checklist of items to bring: swimsuits, sweaters, T-shirts, tank tops, casual day dresses, winter jackets, and mittens. Oh, not to mention the fourteen formal gowns for the show's Rose Ceremonies.

What?!? Is it cold? Is it hot? Is it winter? Where the heck am I going? I couldn't pack all of these items for a WEEKEND getaway . . . let alone a possible two-MONTH stay!

The list of what I was not allowed to bring was almost as long as what I was told to pack, just as on any reality TV show, on which you never see cameras, cell phones, magazines, books, crossword puzzles, or anything that's at all entertainment oriented.

Hmmm . . .

Did I fail to mention that our luggage was also *extremely* limited? I couldn't believe it.

I'm a girl. I have makeup. I have hair stuff. I have shoes. That alone could fill several bags! How do I possibly even begin to make this work?

It all seemed kind of ridiculous, and I was quickly starting to question whether I had made the right decision.

At first, it seemed impossible to overcome the packing challenges, but then I really started thinking about it. As much as I wanted the adventure of going on *The Bachelor,* I wasn't actually going on the show to look for love. I was simply going to move on with my life and find a new, happy place inside of myself. I needed to rediscover me. And since I believed that finding love on the show to be pretty much impossible, I didn't plan on sticking around too long, so I started relaxing about the whole packing dilemma. *Two weeks, tops,* I thought, *is enough time for me to be away.*

It wasn't so much that I thought two weeks would be long enough for me to get over Tye, or that going on *The Bachelor* would help me get over him 100 percent. But I knew that I just needed to get away from Tye, and I thought that even a short stay on the show would give me that nudge I needed to move on, get my feet back on the ground, and regain the sense of independence I'd lost while we were dating.

So that's how I solved my space issues—by literally only packing for about two weeks. I joked with all of my friends that I'd be back by Halloween, so they should hold on to my Halloween costume for me. Even though it was only late September, of course I already had it all planned out. My Madonna "Like a Virgin" costume was ready to go!

Maybe it was because I had so much going on in my personal life at that point that, looking back, I can hardly believe how calm I was about the prospect of appearing on national TV. Now, having been on television, I totally would have approached it differently; maybe bought some nice makeup and learned how to do my hair. But I didn't do much of anything in preparation. I think my mom took me on one quick shopping trip for a few outfits. This meant so much to me, since I knew she wasn't thrilled about my doing the show. It reminded me that she's my mom, and ultimately she'll do whatever she can to make me happy, even if that means supporting me in choices that she doesn't necessarily back. I think that shopping day was her way of saying, "I don't understand or agree with what you're doing, but I love you."

Even so, I didn't really buy that many new clothes. I picked up maybe three tops on our shopping spree, just to make sure that I had enough solid pieces rather than printed or fancy ones, and that was it. I definitely didn't buy any new dresses. Do you know how expensive formal dresses can be?? I had only two, and they were from my junior and senior proms back in 2000 and 2001. One other thing: They were two-pieces. Yeah . . . slight dilemma.

When I wanted to dress up and look cute in Dallas, I sometimes wore little black shorts and a top, so I brought those outfits for the Rose Ceremonies. I was totally oblivious to the fact that some women were actually going to whip out their homecoming and prom dresses, and fix their hair into updos for this thing. And there I was, packing my white shorts and tank tops, thinking I had it all together. My friends, however, made me take a couple of their extra dresses, so I had enough for all of the Rose Ceremonies. They didn't want me to use my lack of dresses as any kind of excuse to come home early.

The truth was, I still had no idea what I was getting myself into. I had only seen a few episodes of *The Bachelor,* and I didn't do ANY research before leaving to be on the show. Early on in college, Stefani and I had organized informal *Bachelor/Bachelorette* Viewing Party nights, but that was a long time ago, back in the Andrew Firestone era. And I hadn't really watched it since. So I vaguely recalled the concept of the show, but none of the specifics. I didn't remember that romantic dates were usually set up out of the country, or that parents got involved. If I had known this last part, I would have spoken to my parents again, one last time, before I left. Instead, I went in blind.

They say that ignorance is bliss. And they're right! All I focused on was the great adventure I was about to embark on that would finally help me climb out of the black hole that I'd been living in for more than six months. I was tired of feeling sad. I was tired of feeling as if I had no control over my emotions. I knew that I was the only one who could make it all better. I was finally doing something to make a change in my life.

The real truth was that until I boarded that plane to leave, Tye remained a powerful force in my life. The last time we saw each other was two nights before I left, at another dinner date at his house. As usual, we talked about everything—except what was really going on between us. Or the fact that I was leaving in just a few days, and that neither one of us knew what would happen while I was on the show or when I'd be back. Instead, as was our usual way, we kept things light. Of course, you may have guessed by now that I could never just leave him without giving him that one LAST opportunity to finally try to win me over! I was not very good with sharing my emotions with Tye (unless, apparently, I was irrationally yelling). So I took the easy way out and wrote it in a card for him that said: "Tye, I don't really know what to say. I know this is an awkward situation, but I hope you understand why I have to go . . . Look at this card if you ever get lonely, and hopefully you'll think of me . . . because I'll be thinking of you."

At this point, I think both of us had already made up our minds that I needed to go, and he didn't really respond to the card (what a shocker!). The whole night had been weird because he didn't seem to really want me there. Whether he was agitated by the fact that I was leaving, or just finished with the night, I could tell he was preoccupied. Finally, after we had sat together in silence for a little while, he spoke.

"Well, I think it's time for you to go now," he said.

When I walked out of his house, the mood between us was very casual—just like two friends saying good-bye. But inside, I was angry and hurt, once again, that he still hadn't fought for me, or even given me the slightest encouragement that I should keep my feelings for him alive while I was away. I had told him that I'd be back in two weeks, but when I left that night, I didn't see or talk to Tye again for nearly two and a half months.

If I had been hoping for something a little bigger and more romantic to happen between us—and, honestly, I'm not sure that I really was by this point—I was so caught up in my final preparations and the building excitement that it was easy to put my disappointment out of my mind and get swept up in the fun.

•

Stefani and Reagan had planned a last night out for me, which was a little weird since they were the only people who knew where I was actually going! Well, not *where* I was going, because even *I* didn't know that; I mean they knew only that I was flying off to be on *The Bachelor*. It was literally a "Good-bye! We Don't Know Where You're Going" Party!

I had invited Tye to my going-away party, but, of course, he didn't come. That brought back all of the memories of me inviting him places, him not showing up, and the two of us then pretending that I had never asked him in the first place. But it was different now. I was getting used to the idea that he wasn't going to be in my life for a while, and I managed to relax and have fun without him there.

My girls and I went out to dinner, and then we went bowling. I was sad to leave my support group—the friends who had kept me as sane as I could be during my heartbreak—and enter this whole new world where I wouldn't know anybody. I wasn't sure I was emotionally strong enough to deal with life without them at this point.

What if the Bachelor mansion was just a girls' drama fest??

I didn't know if I had it in me to deal with any drama right now.

But Stefani and Reagan were great. They kept pulling me aside so that the rest of the guests couldn't hear them, so they could reiterate how cute Jason was, how many friends I was going to make, and how much fun I was going to have. At the end of the night, they gave me a photo album that was filled with pictures of the three of us.

"Don't forget us while you're gone," Stef said.

I laughed. How could I possibly forget them? Plus, I was only going to be gone for two weeks, remember?

But it was still hard to leave. I teared up, thinking about how many things and people I was going to miss when I left.

Finally, I was able to push all of that sadness aside and focus on the positives when my mom drove me to Dallas Fort Worth

International Airport the next morning. I knew that she and my dad still weren't thrilled about my decision, so it meant a lot to me that they still made the effort to take me to the airport. They didn't exactly send me off with a fireworks display or anything like that. But my mom was showing me her support, in her own way, and her parting words to me were very sweet as she hugged me good-bye.

"Please take care of yourself," she said. "Please remember us. And we'll see you in a little bit."

I distinctly remember sitting on the plane, looking out the window, with this feeling that this was something I was really supposed to go and do. It had almost been too easy. There had been no hurdles for me to jump over. In fact, my boss, my parents, my roommate, my friends, and even Tye had all supported me in their own ways, and made it remarkably simple for me to go.

I imagined what was about to happen to my life, and I got excited as I thought about living in a mansion, getting some sun, making new friends, meeting a guy, and living carefree for a little bit. A sudden feeling of peace and calm came over me, as I just sat and smiled.

I have this strange feeling that today is going to change my life forever.
And, little did I know just how right I was . . .

Just like that, a completely new chapter in my life opened. As I was soon to learn, it wasn't just my surroundings and my day-to-day life that had changed, but, really, everything about my reality. Not to mention the way that I thought about love, life, relationships, and, of course, myself.

It was the beginning of a time that I now call the "Bachelor Bubble." I entered a reality unlike any I had ever been in before. An environment that made me feel and act in ways I'd never imagined myself feeling or acting. But at the time, I was very naïve about this world, and so I thought of the whole process as such an innocent adventure.

I flew into Los Angeles International Airport on a Monday, two days before filming was scheduled to begin. I had so many emotions running through my body. On one hand, I couldn't wait to move into the mansion, make new friends, and just have some much needed *fun*. On the other hand, I couldn't stop thinking about that blond-haired, blue-eyed boy back in Dallas. But still, I knew I needed to start a new chapter in my life, and what better time than now? I hadn't spoken with anybody from the show since I'd met with the producers during the last round of auditions, and I had absolutely no clue what I was getting myself into. Oddly enough, I still wasn't nervous; the mystery of it all was part of the excitement!

When I landed at LAX, I walked downstairs to the exit and saw a chauffeur holding a sign with my name on it. That was a new experience for me.

I've never had a driver before! LA is so glamorous!

I was particularly impressed when, after I went down to baggage claim, a paparazzi photographer came scurrying over and started taking pictures of me. He literally chased me and my driver out into the parking lot. I couldn't believe it!

How do they know I'm a cast member? Is this what happens when you're on the show?

I assumed the attention had to be *Bachelor* related. Clearly, he had seen my name and known that I was in LA to film the show. I realized that this was going to be an even crazier experience than I had thought.

When the photographer followed me to the car and forced me to slam the door on him, the driver looked impressed.

"Who are you?" he asked.

Even though I was excited, I knew better than to think I was some big deal.

"I think he mistook me for somebody else," I said. "Because I'm really nobody. Does this happen a lot here?"

The driver then kindly explained another reason for the special attention, and it had nothing to do with me being an overnight celebrity. Apparently, there's a special concierge at LAX who helps only celebrities with their bags, and for some unknown reason, that's who had carried my luggage for me. Maybe he felt sorry for me when he saw me struggling with my two oversized suitcases. Who knows? But when the photographer saw the concierge with me, he must have assumed I was someone. He probably looked at his pictures later and felt sorry that he'd wasted the energy it took to snap them, because, of course, nobody knew or cared who I was at that point. Regardless, it was still a pretty cool way to start my trip! Definitely something to call home about!

Heck, I just got paparazzi'd!

We drove straight to my hotel, which I couldn't tell you the location of if I tried. I'd never been to LA, except for *The Bachelor* audition, and I was actually a little disappointed by my first real view of the city. I don't know if I thought there would be neon lights flashing everywhere, and the word *Hollywood* plastered all over everything, but my impression was that it was kind of average and looked like anyplace else in the world. There were buildings. There were cars. Really, LA was just another city. Except for the infamous Hollywood sign, which was really cool to see in person. And the wildfires!

Let me just tell you, fire is my biggest fear in the world! I live right in the middle of Tornado Alley, and it doesn't worry me at all. But fire, that's a whole other story. And the day I arrived in LA, there happened to be wildfires raging outside the city.

Great.

My initial excitement about LA, which had started with the paparazzi, faded quickly as I smelled the woodsy, smoky fumes that permeated the air outside the car. The driver could tell I was a little nervous about the wildfires, and he did his best to reassure me that we'd be fine. But when I got out of the car at the hotel, it smelled like we were all going down in flames, and that really freaked me out. Call me a bit dramatic, but this was *not* the two-week vacation I thought I had signed up for!

I had a lot of time by myself until the filming began. I stayed in a hotel, and had nothing to do but drown myself in all the thoughts running through my head. I could only go over the possible scenarios so many times, but I had fun imagining what could be. I would sit and practice what I would do the first time I stepped out of the limo. Maybe I would come out and be fun and spunky? Or maybe I would take the shy approach? Or maybe I would just focus on the walk from the limo to Jason and try not to trip.

And then there was the ever important decision of wardrobe. What the heck was I going to wear to the first cocktail party? I had brought a couple options. I had the ever popular cocktail dress, if I decided to play the fun and spunky role. Or I had the long, formal gown if I decided to take a sophisticated approach.

Who the heck am I kidding? Do I really care what I look like or what I'm wearing?

Once I was done playing fantasy and dress up, I looked around my room, and it suddenly seemed very lonely and empty. Well, at least I had the TV, so I had that to keep me entertained. Well, let me be specific: I had the Disney Channel. That was it. I found myself highly engaged in a daylong *Hannah Montana* marathon.

So there I was: alone in LA, watching *Hannah Montana,* and playing dress up with the clothes I had packed. *Is this really the step up from the birthday at Medieval Times that I was looking for? Hmph . . .*

As anyone who's ever been in a situation similar to this, being alone with your thoughts is a dangerous place to be. The more you think, the more your emotions change. I think I spanned the entire emotional spectrum in about three hours, with my thoughts mainly going back to my status with Tye.

Even though I was feeling more and more self-sufficient by the day, there was still a part of me that wanted to check back in with him to see if my newfound independence had impressed him enough to want me back yet. He probably didn't think I'd really go, and I did. Maybe now that I was gone, he missed me.

I know, I know! I was a work in progress. Be patient with me . . .

I couldn't help myself. I called him. It was the middle of the day, so he was at work. He picked up, but he couldn't talk. I told him that I would call him back later in the day, when I knew he'd be off work, because I had something important to ask him. He agreed, and we hung up. I was actually kind of glad he couldn't really talk then; it gave me more time to think about how I was going to ask him what I needed to know.

Even though we'd been through this time and time again, I still couldn't leave well enough alone. I needed to know the answer to the Big Question: Did he even *want* me to come back?

Now, looking back, I know he had basically given me that answer—several times—and clearly, I just wasn't listening. Or actually . . . I just didn't *want* to listen. I think I honestly thought that Tye was just playing the best game of Hard-to-Get. *Again* . . . *I know. . . .*

I watched the clock closely, and once I knew he was done with work, I lifted the phone to my ear. I had butterflies in my stomach as I considered what his response might be. I hesitated for a moment before dialing his number.

But something wasn't right . . . there was no dial tone! *What the heck?* I tried several times, just to be sure, but there was no getting through. Clearly, this was another blaring sign that just whizzed right past me. I should have taken it as a huge signal that that part of my life was over—and this was not the time to revisit it. But no . . .

At the time, I was devastated. Looking back, though, I'm glad I didn't have to deal with his answer. Either way, it would have crushed me. If he had said he wanted me to come home, I would have wanted to leave on the next plane to Dallas. And if he had said that I should stay in LA as planned, it would have been just as painful as hearing him urging me to leave in the first place. And I'm not even sure how it would have affected me if he had told me he wasn't waiting for me. Option A: It would have damaged me even more than I already was, and I would have just moped my way through the Rose Ceremony, probably leading to an early exit. Or, Option B: It would have made me more determined than ever to look my best on the show, and I'd be in it to win it. Just to really show him.

So, regardless of what Tye would have said to me over the phone that afternoon, the whole outcome of the show almost certainly would have been different.

Not that I felt quite that cavalier about it in the moment. I don't know why I kept setting myself up for heartbreak like I did. If I had been totally honest with myself, I would have had to admit that I knew that Tye wasn't going to beg me to come back. I considered myself "damaged goods," and I didn't really believe I deserved more than what I'd had with Tye. I realized I wasn't going into *The Bachelor* with an open heart, because I had left half my heart back at home. I may have thought I was ready for an adventure and a new start, but I was also very hurt and very vulnerable—a dangerous combination that would cause me to cling to anything that might make me feel better.

Clearly, I needed a serious intervention. And that's exactly what *The Bachelor* was. Let me just say, this was one surefire way to get over unrequited love. It took me to a whole different city. I couldn't have any communication with Tye. And I was thrown into a new journey that kept me completely absorbed at all times. It was hard at first, but ultimately, it was very freeing. Of course, at that moment, I still had no idea what was in store for me.

I had no idea how big the audience for *The Bachelor* was, and I wasn't expecting to be one of the girls who people remembered. From past seasons, I knew that no one really paid attention to anyone but the Bachelor or Bachelorette. After that people were always going, "Gosh dang it, who was the blonde one on that one season? The one with the blue eyes?"

So I wasn't overly concerned about how I looked, which was good, because I had just gotten this haircut that I hated. It was an attempt gone awry of having that post-breakup-makeover that's supposed to make you look so much hotter after the breakup than you did before. Mission totally not accomplished. It looked more like a frizzy, Rachel Do from the '90s than hot bombshell I was aiming for. *Awesome.* And I don't think I was in the best shape of my life, either, but I wasn't too concerned about it.

Finally, the first Rose Ceremony day arrived. I had all day to get ready. Of course, I finished really early, just because I had nothing else to do. I did my own makeup. I did my own hair. I got my own dress on. I had decided to wear this long, skintight, strapless black dress that I had borrowed from Reagan. I figured I'd go the sophisticated route. Problem was, it was probably a size too small! But I had decided it made me look elegant and grown up, so I was determined to wear it. Never mind that I couldn't breathe. Never mind that I couldn't walk, so much as waddle. And never mind that I had to sort of lean back to sit down. The dress was a hot mess, and, emotionally, so was I. But I looked good! And, ladies, we all know that's all that matters.

And then, because I had nothing else to do, I stood in front of the full-length mirror in my room and practiced meeting Jason. I looked at my reflection and psyched myself up: *I'm confident. I'm good.*

I worked on what my introduction to him would be like. *Should I talk first? Or wait for him to speak to me? Do I hug him? Or do we shake hands? And what if I trip on the way out? Oh my gosh! What if I'm a complete disaster?!*

I immediately stopped rehearsing and didn't think about anything anymore. It would be easier to just go with the flow and let it happen naturally. I became calm and started to get excited; excited to get out of the room, excited to meet the girls, and excited to meet Jason. I paced around, waiting for the knock on the door that meant we were ready to go.

The anticipation was building, and building, and building! I met the first group of girls when I got into my limo to head to the mansion. I sized them up, having no idea how big a role any of them were about to play in my life.

Wow, they're beautiful.

I was immediately surprised that the girls were actually really nice and sweet. I have to believe we were all running through the same emotions, and it felt good to finally be able to share my feelings with other people! The anxiety I'd had about the night quickly vanished, and I began to legitimately enjoy myself.

Now this isn't so bad! I can totally get along with these girls!

I was just getting used to what it felt like to be there, when I became nervous for a whole new reason.

I'm clearly the underdog. These four women are stunning, not to mention the other twenty women I haven't met yet.

So I decided that my plan of attack would be to just stay in the background and do my thing. I'm definitely not overly aggressive, but I'm no wallflower. I'd also never actively pursued a guy. (Wait: well, I'd never *successfully* pursued a guy!)

As we got closer to our destination, the nerves started to pick up with all of us. Our limo pulled up in front and stopped. I think I felt my heart drop in my stomach. *Here we go . . . No turning back now.*

Meanwhile, I got my first look at Jason, who was standing outside the house. He was standing in front of the house, facing our limo. I'm not sure if he could see us in the back or not, but it was instinct for me to duck out of his line of vision!

Then I looked outside and saw him again. I convinced myself that he was just as terrified.

My heart started beating so hard as I took in all of my surroundings. I suddenly couldn't remember what I had planned to do or say, and I was just positive that I was going to trip and fall as soon as I stepped out of the limo.

And then, before I could psych myself out anymore, the limo door opened. It felt like time had literally stopped. Every second felt like an hour.

I could feel everyone watching me. And, it didn't help my nerves at all that I literally had to unfold myself from my seat because I couldn't get out of the car in the ridiculous dress I had chosen to wear.

So much for taking the graceful route.

When I finally managed to extricate myself from the car, I could barely walk. Long after all of this was over, I had a chance to watch the episode, and I was mortified to see how I walked. I looked like a football linebacker: swinging the same arm with the same foot! Just what most men are looking for in a woman! I'm not sure if it was because of my nerves, or the one-size-too-small dress, but regardless it was not attractive.

I somehow made it to Jason and tried to remember the introductions I had rehearsed. There was nothing casual about it. There was nothing elegant about it. There was nothing romantic about it. The whole situation was awkward. I managed to get through our initial hug. Maybe I had just gotten wrapped up in the show, but I definitely thought he was cute. And he seemed sweet, with this really genuine smile.

It was going pretty well, and then, well, nerves do funny things. When I tried to speak, my voice came out really high pitched, and I forgot everything I had practiced in my room.

"How are you?" Jason asked politely.

"I'm nervous," I said. "I'm not going to lie."

"Where are you from?"

"I'm from Dallas, Texas."

I had a permanent, unusually large grin on my face.

"Dallas, Texas."

"Yeah, I'm a cowgirl."

I'm a cowgirl?!? Did I really just say that??

So much for making a good first impression. I could hardly believe I'd just said that! I was shaking as I walked into the house, and I felt like I had just made a complete idiot out of myself. I was nervous about meeting Jason and having this strange new experience, which I didn't feel like I was handling particularly well. I needed to calm down!

But I did start to loosen up and enjoy myself. My initial reaction had been right on: the girls were all really nice, actually. And I wasn't nervous anymore. As I looked around, I found myself thinking, *If I stay, I could have fun here. This is a beautiful house. These are great girls. And I would love a little vacation.*

There was a time during that first night when we all had to

vote on the girl we thought was least compatible with Jason. Later, when I watched the moment on TV, I was surprised that a couple of them actually said they wanted me to go home, because they were *intimidated* by me. I was really thrown off by that. *I* was the one intimidated by *them*! It's moments like these that made me feel even more grateful for the friendships I formed in the house. To be honest, I couldn't imagine how they could have possibly been intimidated by me. Maybe that's because although I'm a fairly outgoing person, I'm pretty shy, and I tend to keep to myself in new social situations and wait to feel the crowd out. Maybe they mistook my silence for confidence.

I wasn't trying to overly impress Jason that night. If I had, I probably would have worn a different dress that was a little shorter, or spent a little more time on my hair and makeup. I would have whipped out the fake eyelashes. Instead I just wanted to have fun and be myself, and see what could happen. At the same time—let's be honest—I'm sure that a part of me wanted to get his attention. I definitely didn't want to be one of the girls he rejected. Given how low my self-esteem was after Tye, I think I wanted to see if I could get Jason interested in me.

As nonchalant as I was, I was still nervous about the Rose Ceremony. Jason was sending ten girls home, which was nearly half of us, and I hadn't really gotten a chance to talk to him at all. I was hoping our brief encounter had made him interested enough to keep me.

I kept looking around at all the other girls—the beautiful, smart, funny girls he had to choose from—and I suddenly wasn't feeling very confident. It was hard to focus as he called the names of the girls who would be staying:

"Lauren . . ."

"Kari..."

[*Nervous sigh.*]

"Naomi..."

"Natalie..."

"Molly..."

[*Gulp.*]

"Raquel..."

"Stephanie..."

"Melissa..."

He said my name! He said my name! Phewwww!

I walked up to him to get my rose.

"Melissa, will you accept this rose?" he asked.

"Absolutely, thank you," I said.

I could barely focus on the rest of the names he called, but he did also give roses to my new friends Jillian and Erica. After that, we were done. I had made it through my first night on *The Bachelor.* And after all the emotional highs, we were all exhausted.

Even though I hadn't really slept, I didn't feel tired. I think I was running on pure adrenaline. It was so exciting to be there, and I was having fun! I was making friends! Jason was cute! There you have it: The Bachelor Bubble instantly consumed me. Even though, just the day before, I had been planning to go home within the first two weeks, I was now eager to stay and see how long this adventure could last.

To be honest, I didn't think about home at all. I didn't think about my friends. And, finally, and most unexpectedly, I didn't think about Tye.

Six

LIFE IN
THE BUBBLE

At this point, almost everyone had had some one-on-one time with Jason except for me. I was still staying in the background, and I hadn't quite figured out what exactly I was supposed to do. It felt weird to start pursuing him just like that, and it's never been my personality to wear something or do something to make a guy notice me. So I just sat back and watched the other girls in action.

But even though I was laying low, things had already changed for me. I had come onto the show thinking that I wasn't interested in dating Jason—or anyone, really, for that matter. Now that I was there and caught up in the mood of the Bachelor Bubble, I was hoping that Jason would notice me. Ultimately, I think this happened to everyone. And once it got ahold of me, all I wanted was for Jason to realize that he hadn't talked to me yet and pull me aside for some one-on-one time. If he didn't, I'd soon be the only girl he hadn't started getting to know.

All of the other girls seemed to like Jason, and so I was sure that I would, too, once I got the chance to talk to him. He was attractive.

He was nice. He seemed fun. And I wanted him to like me. It was definitely exciting to have someone new to focus on, and it felt good to finally be moving on from my heartbreak over Tye.

But it was hard not to play mind games while in the house. At the first group gathering with all the girls and Jason after the first Rose Ceremony, I found myself thinking that maybe it was a good thing that he hadn't talked to me yet. It could mean that he already knew he really liked me from what he'd seen so far, and so he didn't want to waste his time talking to me when he could be talking to the other girls who he was still iffy about. At the same time, I realized that he could have already decided that I was one of the girls he *wasn't* interested in, and so why waste time on me that he could give to the girls he liked. I really I had no idea where I stood. And in case he wasn't interested in me, I didn't want to pull him away and attempt to woo him when he didn't want to be wooed—at least by me. (Do you how I was making myself crazy?? And it was only the first day!) But whether or not Jason liked me suddenly mattered to me a lot more than I had ever thought it would.

It would have seemed natural for me to be comparing Jason to Tye, but Tye was not in my thoughts at all. I've always had an ability to be very "out of sight, out of mind." And Tye was definitely out of sight. I had someone new to focus on. Plus, I had the other girls to hang out with, a gorgeous mansion to live in, and no work. Life was pretty good, and I wasn't thinking about anything (or anyone) back home.

Well, that's not entirely true (look at me, still lying to myself . . .). During the day, I was so focused on my surroundings and Jason that I didn't have time to think of Tye. It was a great distraction—even if it was a forced one. But during the first few nights at the mansion, when I was all alone right before I fell asleep, my thoughts had no choice but to quickly wonder what Tye was doing. *Did he miss me? Was he wondering what I was doing? Did he even notice that I was gone? Or worse, was he dating other girls?*

I know I had no right to wonder that last question—believe me, I see the irony considering the situation that I was in. But keep in mind, I never intended to go on the show and actually *date*. But those thoughts only crept into my mind when I was all alone, which was pretty rare . . . thankfully. After all, my whole goal of coming was to get *away* from Tye.

I have to be honest though, all thoughts of Tye completely vanished after I had my first date with Jason. That day was a game changer for me . . . actually, looking back, it was a life changer.

When I first found out that I would have a date with Jason, I was so thrilled! *It's about time! I've hardly said anything to him!* But I got nervous at the same time, because now the pressure was on. Technically, I had not been on a first date in . . . years! Keep in mind, that even though I had dated Tye for a year, he never officially took me on a real first date. So I was definitely worried about what to do.

Now it's just going to be us. I have to have things to talk about. But what happens if I don't have anything to talk about, and then we're just stuck there, sitting in silence? Or what if he decides the date is awful, and he doesn't give me the rose at the end?

Back when I had been in the hotel room, I would imagine how our first date would be. It's no secret there's some extravagance to *The Bachelor* dates . . . just a little. I'd hope we'd do something fun like skydiving, because that seemed less scary than having to talk to Jason the whole time. I can't think of better proof that I wasn't lying when I said I was bad at dating: I'd rather jump out of an airplane than make small talk!

Well, thankfully, my wish didn't come true. We had a great romantic date on the beach where we could just talk. Well, it was mainly me talking, and Jason asking questions. He wanted to know where I was from, what I did, what I liked to do, and all of that kind of stuff. As I answered, we started flirting, and all of the sudden it was fun! I laughed a lot, and I actually started to have butterflies. I couldn't believe it! I hadn't expected to like him. And here I was, having a really good time and letting him into a place that nobody had been in for a very long time, because Jason *let* me. He wanted to be let in, so he got to a place that Tye hadn't gotten. I had wanted Tye to go there, but he had chosen not to do so.

The entire date I felt like I was flying on a cloud. I couldn't remember the last time I had felt so happy and relaxed. *Relaxed* being the key word. With Tye, I was almost forcing myself on him, because I wanted him to like me so much. And Jason just seemed to like me for me . . . I didn't have to force anything. *So this is what a normal date is supposed to feel like, huh? This is how it feels when someone genuinely cares about getting to know me?*

Our date ended, and that was it for me . . . I was hooked. I had fallen victim to the process I had been so cynical about. And I was definitely smitten. Jason had a side to his personality that I hadn't seen from Tye. Jason seemed really sweet. He had been married before, so I knew he wanted to be in a relationship. I started looking at the qualities he possessed that Tye didn't (or, at least, hadn't let me see). *Now, this is the guy I need. Not the twenty-six-year-old who I used to date who didn't know how to be in a relationship, but this grown-up man who really, really, wanted to find love and make a commitment.*

This was a huge turning point for me, and it was obvious on the show. In my profile photo for *The Bachelor,* I had worn a red halter top and a heart necklace that Tye had given me. I wore the necklace as a sign to Tye that even though I was gone, I was thinking about him. And it was a bit of a security piece for me. I kept it on for the first couple days we were in the house. And then, after my first one-on-one date with Jason, I took off the necklace and didn't wear it again the rest of the time I was on the show.

I honestly didn't think much of it at the time, but looking back, it's pretty apparent that I was sending a clear personal signal that I was moving on. I had very quickly converted from Tye mode to Jason mode and *Bachelor* mode. Jason seemed to like me, and suddenly I realized that other people could like me. I wasn't a leper who couldn't get anybody, after all. And it felt really good.

So, emotionally, I was very quickly in a much different place than I had been when I first went on the show. I was very absorbed by this new world. The girls. The amazing dates. And, of course, the new guy. After I took off Tye's necklace, I wasn't thinking about him or home at all anymore. And that's exactly what I had come on the show for . . . I just hadn't expected it to work. I didn't believe in the process, and I didn't believe that anything could get my mind off Tye. And somehow, in one day, my entire belief system changed.

I'd just come from a place where I was working nine-to-five at a job I couldn't stand. And was heartbroken. And miserable. Now I was living this nice, luxurious life with a bunch of good girlfriends, and we were having so much fun. It was like a fantasy come true. I didn't have any reason to think of the sadness back home.

As quickly as my feelings developed for Jason, I never stopped to think that maybe it was *too* soon. I had, in one date, developed a very strong emotional connection that would have taken much longer to develop in the real world. Maybe it was the competition aspect of it all. Maybe it was the vulnerable state that I was in when

I came. Maybe it was a combination of everything, but all I had to think about now was Jason.

But, as natural as it felt at the time, when I look back, I honestly think that the Bachelor could be *any* guy, and the girls would all swoon over him. We all had this idea that if he's the Bachelor, he's got to be pretty perfect or at least have a pretty impressive personal résumé! It almost gave him this special aura and appeal. It also didn't hurt that the romantic dates we went on were so over the top and amazing that they could make anyone seem appealing.

As far as Jason was concerned, I think we all fell for the superficial things about him at first: He was cute, he was a great dad, he was sweet to all of us, and he seemed a bit shy, which was really endearing. Then, once I got to know him deeper than those surface qualities, I liked Jason for who he was around me. I'll be honest: We didn't have a whole lot in common. We liked similar things, like the outdoors and kids. But our conversations didn't go much deeper than that at first. The main attraction for me was just how I felt when I was with him. As I said about Tye, sometimes it just clicks with people and sometimes it doesn't. And with Jason, it clicked (or at least I *thought* it did). At least in the beginning. He made me feel special. He remembered all of the little stories that I told him about my life. He laughed at my jokes. He just made me feel so good.

Looking back, though, I realize that I didn't know a whole lot about him. Nor did I ever get to know him on a deeper level, because I was the one who did most of the talking. Jason would ask me a question, and I would answer him, or tell a story, and then just keep talking. Never once did it occur to me that maybe I should be asking him questions, or that I should be trying to get to know him as much as he was trying to get to know me. I let my emotions run ahead of my rational side. Now I can see that I just wanted so badly for Jason to like me that I never asked myself, *Do I really like him? Do I even know anything about him?*

And oddly enough, it never struck me as abnormal that I was one of twenty-five women fighting for a guy. I mean, seriously, would this ever happen in Dallas? Sorry, but even if it were Tye back home and twenty-five women were all vying for his affection, I would wave my white flag and bow out—that's just too weird of a situation. So why did it never feel that way when I was in the mansion?

As time went on though, the process got very difficult for me. The more emotionally invested I got in Jason, the harder it was to see him with other girls. Obviously. Whenever we were in group settings, it was so hard for me to act normal. Jason and I had made such a great connection on our first date and had our own inside jokes and stories, but I couldn't exactly bring those up in a group situation. So I sat back and observed. It was hard to see him flirting with the other girls. Who did he seem to like the most? Talk to the most? Laugh with the most? It was very difficult not to overanalyze the situation.

Who can blame me? I mean, in what normal society would you be expected to be okay to watch the person you're dating do this stuff with other people? *Twenty-five other people!*

Group dates were the most brutal to watch. I was forced to watch him and see the connections that he'd made with all the other girls. And it made the confidence that I'd had in our relationship dwindle. I suddenly began to feel very weak again.

Am I setting myself up for heartbreak again? Did Jason not feel the same way about me as I did about him? Should I bow out and leave before he gets a chance to reject me?

It wasn't that I really wanted to go home, because I did genuinely care about Jason. The hard part at that point was that a bunch of the other girls really liked him, too. Navigating all of these intense feelings was a lot harder than I had thought it would be. Here I was, emotionally invested in someone, and other people felt the same way about him, too. And this guy that we all liked, he was the one who had the control over whether he and I would be together in the end, or whether he'd end up being with someone else. It was a real mind trip.

On top of that, it scared me that I had such strong feelings for Jason right after I had just left what I thought was such a great relationship. And when I really thought about it, as much as I liked the way that I was feeling, I didn't understand how, in a week and a half, I could have met someone who gave me butterflies and made me want to stay and fight for him.

One by one, the other girls got eliminated. We went from fifteen to twelve to nine to five. And the fewer people who were left, the more I found myself thinking, *Please, please, please, don't let it be me who goes home.*

I have to admit that, in some way, I was really surprised by everybody who got sent home, because I had no way of knowing what he was looking for or who he liked. But I'll be honest, during the Rose Ceremonies, I wasn't thinking too much about the other girls. I was mostly waiting to hear my name be called. And I never singled out a girl and thought it should be her turn to go home on a particular night.

With nothing else to think about, and my future happiness seemingly at stake, I became paranoid and overanalyzed every little thing that happened. There really was no moment where I felt 100 percent confident. I was riding another emotional roller coaster, and it was starting to make me dizzy.

But when it was just the two of us, I was so happy. It was easy to talk to Jason. And we weren't just making small talk, either. He wanted to know about my parents, and my family, and everything about my life before *The Bachelor*. The questions he asked, and the way he asked them, made me think that he liked me as much as I liked him.

I was still the one mainly answering *his* questions. It never occurred to me to ask if this is what *I* wanted, I just assumed it was. Sure, I didn't know a lot about him. And sure, I was doing most of the talking. But he seemed to like *me*. And that's all I wanted . . . it's what I needed.

I had convinced myself that if this worked out, I'd just up and move to Seattle (where Jason lived). I had nothing keeping me in Dallas. My friends and family were there, but they weren't going anywhere, and so I could easily go back and see them anytime. I really thought that it wouldn't be that hard to enter into this relationship with Jason and just start over in a new city. By this point, I really cared about him, and I thought this was where I was supposed to be, right here with him, wherever that happened to be. As far as I was concerned, God had taken me out of my situation at home and brought me here, and this was the new path that I was supposed to be on. And so I was giving it everything I had.

What I didn't realize at the time was that I was inside the Bubble, and so it never dawned on me that I might not be living in reality. I never questioned that I could fall in love in two weeks. I never once wondered what was going on back home or thought about what my life after the show would be like in any real way. I felt like this was my life now. *This was my reality.* And it was very easy to extend that fantasy to what might happen if Jason chose me at the end of the show. It was very exciting to think that when this was all over, if I was with Jason, I could move to Seattle, knowing that I had finally found what I was looking for, and I could have my own life—get my own job, make my own friends, and do my own thing—in a way I hadn't felt able to in Dallas since Tye and I had broken up.

By the time there were only five of us left, I was sure that Jason and I had a connection that went above and beyond what he shared with anyone else. For one thing, I definitely had spent the most alone time with him out of everybody. Now, I understand that in the real world, a girl usually needs more signs than this to believe that she's met her future husband—hence my constant references to the Bubble. But here, this was all I needed to make me think that Jason was really interested in me and in our relationship. And that felt real to me.

I did have a huge "reality check" moment though, when I found out that my mom and dad were refusing to take part in the upcoming hometown dates. A part of me wasn't surprised. I knew they didn't believe in the show or support my involvement in it. Only now it was a little different, because I wanted them to meet the man I loved— and hoped would be their future son-in-law—on national TV.

I was devastated to hear they wouldn't participate. I had gotten so wrapped up in the Bachelor Bubble that I didn't understand their reaction.

Why don't they understand that I'm falling in love with this person? Why don't they want to meet him? Don't they know that he won't propose to me if they don't meet him? Why are they being so gosh darn difficult?

I was upset and hurt that they didn't want to be a part of something so big in my life. I was also terrified that if Jason couldn't meet my family, it would push him away. And, beneath the surface, I was starting to get confused about what was "real."

Are my parents right? Is this silly? Is everyone back home laughing at me for thinking I'm in love? No! They just don't understand! If they were in my shoes, they'd be feeling the same way that I do—wouldn't they?

I wasn't so sure. Hearing my parents' protest had momentarily popped my Bachelor Bubble. I suddenly wondered if everybody else at home doubted the show, too, and thought I was being silly and stupid for letting it get this far. I teetered on the edge of doubt. But then I blocked it out again.

There was still a big part of me that thought this was all very real, particularly my feelings for Jason, and I didn't want to hear anything to the contrary from anybody, not even my own family. I assumed they was wrong because they simply didn't understand how genuine my feelings for Jason were and how genuine his feelings for me seemed to be.

Just like that, my Bubble was my reality again. And in my Bubble, I was upset with my parents and despondent that they might have hurt my chances with Jason. This could be my true love, and they didn't want to meet him or be a part of my exciting new life.

At the time, it never crossed my mind that every single finalist came home in love with Jason after a date. I didn't question why or how, but looking back, I really don't understand what happened to make all these intelligent, rational women react so strongly. I mean, I doubt that Jason was at home after every one of these dates thinking he was so in love with each of us.

I definitely was starting to get emotionally exhausted. The highs and lows were so extreme. But as intense as the past month had been, and as close to the edge as I sometimes felt, I was still very much hanging on to try to win Jason's heart. I didn't want to go home. But the process was draining!

Emotionally, I was a wreck! Everything revolved around Jason and who he liked, who he dated, who appeared to be winning most of his attention—and it just drains you after a while. So, for me, I felt that *on top of* the emotional drama I'd been through for the six months prior to going on *The Bachelor*. I don't think I really had any control over my emotions at the time, but while I was living it, I felt completely in control for the first time. Oh the irony. My Bachelor Bubble had created a safety net for me: a place where I felt in control of my feelings; a place where I felt safe. But in reality, that couldn't have been farther from the truth.

seven

·

IN LOVE . . .
AND OUT
OF CONTROL

My parents' decision to not participate had definitely made me question things about my new life. To be honest, I had completely forgotten about things at home. Obviously not my friends and family, but I forgot about my old life. And it did make me wonder what people were thinking back home. If they were making fun of me, if they were proud of me, if they were laughing at me.

Thankfully, I got my answer on the hometown dates. Since my parents were not involved, we got to meet up with several of my friends. I was actually a little relieved about this. My friends were more open-minded about everything, and they wouldn't be as intimidating to defend my position to.

Surely they'll be honest! They'll let me know if what I've found is real, or if they're teasing me for actually believing that I'd found love.

And the date went great! I was so comforted after visiting with my friends. The group date went as smoothly as it could have. My friends were the people who had seen what an emotional mess I was before I left for *The Bachelor,* and they could clearly see a change in my demeanor now. And that was all thanks to Jason and my new-found confidence.

At one point, Stefani and I were on her bed talking, and I told her how I felt and how in love I was, and how happy I was. She immediately started crying. Her emotional response to meeting Jason was a huge indication for me that this relationship was the right thing for me. My friends were the ones who had clarity regarding the situation, and if they were happy, then this clearly had to be the right path for me. They didn't like Tye. But they loved Jason. And I finally felt like I had it all.

On top of that, I liked Jason more and more. And after my home visit, our relationship kind of felt official. He had met my friends. It seemed like they approved, and everybody seemed really happy. *This is what it would feel like if we were a real couple, and we came to Dallas to visit my friends!* After the eight months I had just endured, that was a huge moment for me.

It was the happiest I had been in a long time. I had a confidence in me that I think I lost while dating Tye. My world with Jason just seemed so much easier. And what blew me away was that he just seemed to like *me*. I didn't really find myself fighting for his attention. I can't tell you how good it felt to finally have someone care about me in that way—it was something I had wanted for so long.

We were getting closer and closer to the end of the process. And I wanted nothing more than for it to be over. I wasn't sure if Jason had doubts. But at this point, I didn't have any. I felt certain that I was supposed to marry him. No matter how much I wanted to feel loved after everything I had been through, I never in a million years would have accepted a proposal from somebody I didn't think I was

100 percent in love with. Now I just had to see if he felt the same way about me.

There was one small problem with my dream: There were still three of us girls left. And they were girls who I really liked and respected. It would have been so much easier if I hadn't bonded with them, but unfortunately that wasn't the case. But I had to stay focused on me and Jason. After all, it was a competition. And I was determined to win the chance to spend the rest of my life with the man I loved. Because they were friends of mine, I couldn't let myself think about what they were doing or how they were feeling. The few times my mind went there, it was like emotional overload, and I realized it was not a healthy place to be. What worked for me instead, was my good old "out of sight, out of mind" philosophy. If I didn't have to see them interacting, I was fine. I really was.

So there we were, the final three girls, and we were heading to New Zealand! I had never been out of the country, except for a vacation to Mexico, but never anywhere as exciting as New Zealand! I think our exotic destination was almost as exciting to me as the fact that I had made it to the next round. My life seemed absolutely perfect. And I just got to go along for the ride!

Emotionally, I was in a really good place. I had gone through several highs and lows throughout the process, but I had finally reached some stability. I thought I had found *the guy*. I thought I was in love. I thought I was happy. I mean really, genuinely happy. Marriage was a very big deal for me, and I was sure it was about to happen in my life. Maybe I had taken an unconventional path, but it was the one I had found, and I knew that I was totally where I was meant to be. And the concept of marriage was becoming a very real possibility very quickly. I mean, that was the point of this whole process, right? And the end was not too far off.

My thoughts began to venture off into what my life would be like. Keep in mind, I had not been in my "real life reality" in quite some time. I had been living in my world with Jason of lavish dates and exotic vacations. And when I imagined our future together in this world in my mind, everything would work out perfectly.

My dates with Jason were coming to an end. I only had a handful of them left before the whole experience was going to be over. But I didn't feel any pressure, just confidence. Oddly enough though, I always made sure I had conversation topics in my head before we'd have a date together. Just in case the conversation reached a lull I wanted to be the one to have a funny story to bring us back on track. It didn't strike me as odd that I would go on our dates with a checklist of things to talk about, just to keep the conversation going. I knew my time with him was limited, and I wanted to make sure it wasn't filled with awkward silence. (Should have been a red flag . . . but I think we've established that I'm not very good at picking up signs.)

Our conversations seemed to flow so easily because I had no problem telling Jason how happy he made me, and how I hadn't felt this way in a long time. Never mind that ordinarily I wasn't the kind of girl who said stuff like that. Or that it had taken me over a year to say anything like that to Tye. Things happened fast in the Bachelor Bubble, and while I was living that reality, all of this emotion just kind of came out of me. So much of our conversations were me spilling my heart and my feelings out all over Jason.

I distinctly remember the night that I said those "three little words" that we're always warned about saying. I didn't just throw that word around either. And the last time I said it, I got a blank stare as a response. But that night, I just felt like I had to say it. I really felt like I was in love—I was in a place I'd never been before—and I wanted him to know!

I remember we were sitting on a couch in New Zealand, and it just came out. "I'm falling in love with you."

Now, I knew he couldn't say it back, even if he felt it, but it was still hard to say those words to someone and not hear anything back. Especially, since this would be the second time I'd said that to someone, just to have him not say it back. But at least this time, I could convince myself that Jason really wanted to say it back, he just couldn't. It's no secret the Bachelors can't reveal their true feelings until that very final moment. So I would just have to wait until then to see if he felt the same.

But his reaction was to hug me tight and kiss me. *I believe that's a good sign.*

That was a huge moment for me. I had not only admitted to myself, but also admitted to Jason just how deep my feelings were. And there was no turning back after those words are said! You can't retract them. But I was glad I had said it, and I had gotten a good reaction to them. Now, he knew exactly where I was emotionally, and didn't have to wonder if I was really in this.

By this time, there were only two of us left, me and Molly. I had really forgotten that it was still a competition at this point. I felt like Jason was my boyfriend, and I was his girlfriend. But I was not so naïve to block out the obvious. Deep down, I knew what was at stake. And whenever I thought about possibly losing this new love that I'd found, I got a huge pit in my stomach. So I forced myself to just think about the positive.

After meeting Jason's family, I was even more convinced we were supposed to be together. They were so warm and inviting, and they genuinely seemed interested in trying to get to know me. And to me, this was the last real hurdle to making our romance official. It was the final step in this process.

This was it: the last official time we would get to be together before Jason had to make the decision to be with me, or not. No pressure or anything, right?

I remember the last time Jason left me before the final Rose Ceremony. We had just had our final date, and I wouldn't see him again until he was either proposing to me, or rejecting me. I didn't want him to leave. As confident as I pretended to be, I was terrified about the possibility of losing this new love. The next time we talked, he could very well be saying good-bye to me forever.

Things that made sense to me in my Bubble don't make sense to me anymore. There were huge issues that I just ignored and didn't think about. How could I become *engaged* to someone who had been dating multiple women the entire time? Could he really, truly love me if he was dating someone else? And why was I okay with the fact that he had all the control? I had found someone I loved, and that I wanted to be with . . . but the decision to be together wasn't up to me. I had no control over whether or not we'd be together.

And these thoughts brought Tye right back into my mind. Not because I missed him or was wondering what he was doing, but because my current situation suddenly began to mirror my old one. I was in love and out of control of the situation . . . again.

The day was finally here, the day for which I'd waited two months, and which would decide my future forever. My mind went back and forth the entire time I was getting ready. I felt confident that I was about to receive a proposal.

Surely, he's going to pick me. How could he not, after the connection that he and I have made? What about all of the little signs he gave me that showed how much he cared? This is it. It has to be!

Then it wouldn't be long before my mind went in the other direction.

But what if he doesn't pick me? I mean, I'm sure Molly is feeling just as confident as I am right now. What if I'm the girl he sends home? What if he does care about me, but he cares about her more? I didn't even think about that.

Let the mind games continue. You can see why I was so emotionally drained after going through an experience like this. And reliving it makes me just as dizzy!

•

On the limo ride over to the proposal destination, my heart began to pound. It sounded like a drum line was performing right next to me. I mean, I had thought about the possibility of being rejected, but I hadn't *thought* about it . . . and now I was . . . and now was *not* the time!

Wait! I'm not ready yet! I need to get my emotions in check!

I had no idea whether I was the first girl, or the second, or if anything had happened yet, or what was going to happen when I did finally get to Jason. I was trying to catch my breath, but I was too nervous. I was trying to smile, but my lips were quivering at the edges of my mouth. My hands were sweaty. I was concentrating on trying not to trip or let my fear and longing show on my face.

Should I look at him? Should I avoid eye contact?

I had been so confident up until now, but I suddenly felt very awkward, maybe because it had sunk in that it was a real possibility that he might reject me. I didn't want to make eye contact with him and possibly read his expression before I got to him.

When I finally reached Jason, he smiled at me, grabbed my hands and gave me a small kiss. I took a deep breath.

Here we go.

We stood there for a moment, just looking at each other. His face was impossible to read.

Was he happy? Was he nervous that he was about to reject me?
He smiled slightly.

"Our very first date, I started falling for you," he said. "From the blimp ride, to meeting your friends, seeing you with Ty, seeing you with my family, seeing it all."

Oh my gosh! Oh my gosh! Unless there's a big but *coming soon, this is really good!*

Jason started smiling a little bigger, and I slowly started to smile back. He grabbed my hands tighter.

"I came into this looking for someone exactly like you," he said. "Exactly like you. I said to myself early that throughout all this, I don't know if I could ever say good-bye to you."

I was looking at him now, and I knew this was it! He was picking me!

My heart suddenly started to fill up, and I couldn't keep the biggest smile from taking over my whole face. I wanted to fall into his arms at that very moment.

"You make me happier than I've ever been in my entire life," he said. "I've wanted to tell you something for a long time now: I'm completely in love with you!"

I shrieked. It was a noise that I didn't even know I could make! I immediately started jumping up and down and hugging him—I was so unbelievably happy! I had found what I was looking for. I loved him, and he loved me! I was loveable again, and it felt so good!

And then, Jason got down on his knee and proposed to me.

Unreal! This was the moment that I had been waiting for my entire life.

Of course I accepted. I was in a cloud of total happiness. I had made it to the end. I had won. I had gotten my man. I had found true love! We were going to be a family! I was so content that I had found the right place for me.

Jason really did fill all of the holes where things had been missing in my previous relationship with Tye. I hadn't had any of that good romantic attention since the early days of my relationship with Josh, and that had been when I was a teenager. It felt as good to receive such attention as I had imagined it would feel during the many long nights I had been alone before *The Bachelor*.

And just like that . . . it was all over. I was in love, I was engaged, and I was going back home to my real world. I was confident our relationship would work—even though I didn't really think of *how* it would work . . . I just assumed it would. We were happy, in love, and getting married. It just had to work out.

The Bachelor Bubble still had a powerful hold on me, and when we left New Zealand to go home, I was still giddy. I was so happy that I had found this man who I loved, who loved me too, and now we were going to get married and start a life together. The only downside was that I couldn't celebrate with anyone, since the world didn't know yet. But that was all right. I figured it would give Jason and me more time to get to know each other before our good news became public.

Jason and I said our good-byes in New Zealand, and I headed back home. It took a little adjusting to get back to normal again. I hadn't been home in a long time, and I hadn't talked to anyone in weeks, so I was anxious to see what I had missed. First things first, I turned my phone on to get all my missed emails and messages.

I turned on my phone while waiting in line at security, and it *blew up*! Honestly, it was a little overwhelming.

Before I had left for *The Bachelor*, my first thought would have been to immediately check to see if Tye had left me a message. But

I had finally accepted that he had never cared about me in the same way that I had cared about him. I was happy to now be giving my love to someone who wanted it and had love to give me in return. I knew that Tye hadn't called me while I was gone, and at that point, I didn't really even care.

Literally one minute after I turned my phone back on (the messages were actually still downloading), it rang. I looked down at the screen.

It was Tye.

My heart stopped for a minute. I was surprised that he was calling me, but more than that, I was struck by how much I had changed. For the first time, ever, I honestly didn't want to talk to him; not after everything he'd put me through.

I hit Ignore.

Huh, look at that. That felt pretty good.

Immediately after I hit Ignore, I got a text message.

Again from Tye.

"Where have you been? What are you doing?"

He must have known I was back when my phone didn't go straight to voicemail.

I didn't call him back or return the text message. I had come home a new person. I was confident. I had found myself again. I had felt what it was like to be loved again. I wasn't sad anymore. I wasn't heartbroken. And I was downright angry with Tye. And I didn't want to have anything to do with him.

Scrolling through my text and voice messages, I saw that most of them were from Tye. And they dated back to the week I left for the show.

Pretty much every message I had waiting for me on my voicemail was also from Tye. He sounded so sad and pathetic. But I wasn't moved. After the first few messages, I stopped listening to them and just hit Delete. I didn't want to hear it. Not now. I felt so happy with how independent I had become, all that I had gone and done, and the new relationship that it had led me to find. And, looking back at Tye, I couldn't believe that I had let that disaster of a relationship drag on for eighteen months.

Whenever I thought about the past, I got mad at Tye all over again for treating me as badly as he had for so long. I didn't think he'd really changed. I figured he only wanted to talk to me now because he couldn't. And if he thought he wanted me back, it was only because he couldn't have me. I honestly didn't have anything to say to him. I had said everything I needed to say before I left.

And things were different now. The experience of going away had given me exactly what I needed, which was to get away from him and get back onto my own two feet again, so I could finally look at the relationship without my heart goggles on. I saw what my friends had seen all along. It had never been a healthy relationship. Now that I could see that, and I was in a new, committed relationship—and even more important, a new mental state—I didn't want to risk falling back into that unhealthy cycle again. And so I decided to avoid Tye.

The only person I wanted to hear from at that point, anyhow, was Jason. I was over the moon about our engagement. I had gone into *The Bachelor* expecting absolutely nothing, and now I had come home with everything I could have wanted. I was with this new great guy. I had a whole new life ahead of me. And I was excited to embark on everything that was waiting for me.

I had been away for two months, and I was happy to see everybody and share the little bit of my news that I could. My parents were aware that I was engaged, and my friends figured it out pretty quickly. I never said anything to them, but they knew me well enough to be able to tell. For starters, I was obviously in a very different place emotionally. When I left for *The Bachelor,* I was so broken, and I didn't want to talk to anybody. And when I came back, I felt on top of the world. And everyone could see that.

When I first got home to Dallas, Jason and I talked on the phone a couple of times a day and texted each other almost constantly. I was still giddy about our engagement, and I was always excited when his name came up on my phone.

Things changed very quickly, though. The conversations soon grew much shorter, and shallower. We didn't seem to have a whole lot to talk about. And I found myself planning out things to tell him, like I had done in New Zealand. I had figured that once we were back in the real world, our relationship would just fall into place. But it just didn't feel as natural as I had hoped. This made me nervous, but I was still willing to fight for us. I had made this commitment and accepted a proposal from Jason. I had to make it work.

Not only that, but Jason and I were both well aware of the reality of the show: Out of all of the seasons of both *The Bachelor* and *The Bachelorette,* only one couple had ever made it last. Jason and I had even laughed about the poor odds during our first days together, when we were sure we were going to be the second couple to survive. Now, I wasn't so sure. But it would be so humiliating to become just another statistic and pop culture joke. And so I kept telling myself that things would get better. I made excuses for Jason: He was busy because he had a young son to take care of, and because he was about to start promotion for *The Bachelor.* I also resolved to try harder to create the good relationship I thought I had found.

Only, it wasn't easy. Even when Jason and I did talk on the phone, it wasn't just relaxed conversation between us while we got caught up in the rush of getting to know each other. This should have been the time when we were on the phone from eight o'clock at night until midnight: We barely knew each other, we were in love, and we should have been so excited to find out everything about each other as fast as we possibly could. The questions should have been flying:

"What's your favorite color?"

"What do you like to cook?"

"What trips do you want to take?"

"Where do you see yourself in five years?"

But there was none of that. In fact, it seemed like Jason never had a lot to say about anything. Many times when we were on the phone, we really did sit there in awkward silence for what felt like minutes at a time. What I started to realize was that Jason and I had very different personalities. I'm very outgoing and bubbly. I'm a smart aleck. I tell jokes. But I didn't feel like I could be myself, and when I did, I started to feel like I was doing more of the talking than he was.

One of my big things, which I had done with Tye, too, was to send jokes via text. Just little silly things to brighten his day. I started doing this for Jason. Only, Jason never really understood them. Not only that, but when I said something that I thought was clever and funny, it often wouldn't really get the response from Jason that I was expecting. This left me at a total loss as to what I could possibly do to make things better. But I knew that if we were so confident in our love while we were newly engaged in New Zealand, we would definitely make it work back home.

Making things more difficult for me, Tye was still in the picture, and not because I was the one instigating anything, either. He was constantly calling and texting me. All of his messages went unanswered, but he was relentless. There had been a time when this kind of attention and concern from Tye would have made me jump up and down with happiness. But not now. Not when I was engaged to someone else. Not when I'd had the chance to finally get some much-needed perspective on Tye. He would send texts:

"Where are you?"

"What are you doing?"

"Why are you ignoring me?"

"Why are you not picking up?"

In my head, I would respond, *Because I don't want to talk to you right now.*

Heck, he knew what it meant when someone ignored someone else. He invented that game! Had he forgotten that he was the one who taught me how to play?

In real life, though, I didn't respond at all.

But I couldn't just ignore him forever. This was Tye, after all. Given how crazy he used to make me, it's hard to believe that I was as strong as I was for so long. I think my disinterest in talking to him shows just how deeply he hurt me. And I also think it's a testament to how serious I was about my commitment to Jason and how determined I was to make our relationship work, if there was any hope for us at all.

I didn't tell anyone—including Tye, of course—that I had won *The Bachelor* or that I was engaged to Jason. By not responding to Tye, I was trying to let him know that I had another priority in my life now, and that he couldn't keep coming at me like he was. I didn't know what to do. The last thing I wanted, after taking such a great step forward, was to make a huge mistake, take ten steps back, and end up right where I had been eight months before. And so, I literally spent several weeks analyzing everything that was happening in my life and what I should do about it.

After two or three weeks of Tye texting and calling me nonstop, I finally picked up his call one night. I don't know what was different for me at that particular moment, but I think it had finally sunk in that he wasn't giving up, and that maybe his persistence had earned him a chance to talk to me. I was sitting on the floor in my bedroom reading up on all the magazines that I'd missed while I was gone. I answered the phone confidently, but I was unsure about how the conversation would go.

I cleared my throat.

"Hello?" I said.

There was a slight pause from the other end of the phone. Maybe he was shocked that I actually picked up.

"Hey," he said awkwardly.

I flipped the page of my magazine.

"Hey."

We went through a bunch of small talk, and the inevitable "How are you?" and "What have you been up to?"

When I asked Tye how he'd been, he let it all out.

"Well, I've missed you," he said. "I thought about you a lot, and thought about our relationship a lot."

"Mmmm-hmmm," I muttered.

I was still flipping through my magazine as he continued.

"I, um, I'm sorry for how we left things," he said. "I had a lot of time to think about things, and I owe you an apology."

Well, yes you do! Sheesh.

I sighed and studied a picture in the magazine.

"Oh really? Why?" I asked.

I wanted to hear him say it. I needed to hear him say it.

"I just . . . I don't think I gave us a fair shot," he said. "And I'm sorry."

I felt the urge to say everything to him that I'd been hiding for the past year and a half. I had gone from being sad over Tye to being mad at Tye. I no longer feared telling him what I was really thinking, because I wasn't scared of losing him anymore. *Heck, he wasn't mine. I had moved on. I was happy. So what did I have to lose, right?*

"You're right. You didn't give us a fair shot," I said. "But if we were meant to be together, we would be together. It was just too hard of a relationship. It shouldn't be that hard. It just wasn't meant to be."

Wow. That actually felt really good to say.

I had no idea I had become this confident. But I finally had the guts to say everything I had been afraid to say for so long, and I intended to be honest and tell him exactly where I was at in my life.

"You're right," he said. "If we were meant to be, we'd be together."

Ouch.

Even though I had said the words first, I didn't expect him to agree with me. Part of me wanted him to keep fighting for me. But a larger part of me was relieved that this cycle finally looked like it was over. We had both agreed that a relationship between us would never work. So I continued on with my final conclusion of that relationship.

"For the past year and a half, you took me for granted," I said. "You didn't appreciate me. You have no idea the things I did for you. My life revolved around you, and I got nothing back. You made it too hard for me."

"You're right," he said quietly.

I didn't know how to react to that.

Wait a minute, that's not what you're supposed to say. You're the bad guy. Be the bad guy!

After a short pause, he continued.

"I really missed you while you were gone," he said. "I really care about you, and I want you to be happy."

I heard the words, but I felt nothing. Even though it was exactly what I had longed to hear him say for so many months, it was too late now. I didn't want to listen. So I tuned him out. The little bit that did get through to me just made me mad. At one point, he told me how hard the past couple of months had been for him, and it made me want to laugh and say, "What about how hard the past *year* has been for me?"

Not only was I angry enough to feel like it was well within my rights to be a borderline brat, but I had moved on. Of course, contractually, I wasn't allowed to tell Tye that. Heck, I didn't even want to tell him that. It was none of his business that I had moved on after we'd broken up. Isn't that just to be expected?

We talked for a little longer. I continued to tell him everything that had bothered me both during and after our relationship. And he continued to listen and agree with me. It felt so good to be this confident with him and to speak so honestly. At the end of the conversation, I just sighed. This was it.

"Okay, well, I wish you well," I said.

Maybe that's not the nicest thing to say to someone you were so in love with, but how else do you really end an awkward conversation after that love has been stamped out?

"Let's try and stay in touch, and I hope we can be friends some day," I said. "Right now, I just don't see that in our future, though."

There was a long pause before he answered.

"Okay, take care," he said. "And I really do hope you're happy."

"Good-bye, Tye."

I hung up the phone and closed my magazine.

Did that really just happen? Did we just have the "good-bye" conversation?

"Good-bye, Tye" had been a phrase I had feared for so long. But it had flowed right out of me. I honestly thought that was the final contact between Tye and I. It was a strange feeling. You never forget someone you used to love so much. But sometimes, you have to accept you were not meant to be. And that's exactly what we had just done.

Even if it was clear that things weren't going that well with Jason as soon as I left the Bachelor Bubble, it was hard for me to let go of how good he had made me feel while I was in the world of the show with him. There had been a time when I had made Jason laugh, and he had thought I was beautiful. He had given me all of those little smiles, and winks, and kisses. He had chosen me out of twenty-five beautiful, accomplished women and put a ring on my finger, signaling his intention to spend the rest of his life with me. All of that attention had built up my confidence to where I could see myself as an intelligent, attractive, self-sufficient woman.

I finally believed that I deserved to have somebody treat me well rather than being with someone who I had to force to like me. I always felt like I had to constantly remind Tye that I was worth loving. Jason didn't need reminding; he had made me feel like he cared about me all on his own. I realized that I didn't need much out of a relationship; I just wanted someone to step up and love me like I deserved to be loved. I had that now. (Err . . . so I thought . . .).

Just because Tye had missed me when I went away did not make up for the year when he had acted like I wasn't good enough for him. Then there were all of the things I had done to win Tye's heart: all of the meals, coffees, laundry, and more. I hadn't had to do any of that for Jason, and he had still picked me to be his wife. Of course, I hadn't yet had the chance to even begin to have a normal relationship with Jason, so it was clearly crazy for me to try to compare the two.

Aren't love goggles great?

But there was one definite connection between the two men: The fact that Jason had built up my confidence was making it easier for me to say no to Tye. I was determined to try to hold on to my relationship with Jason instead.

The problem was that things continued to get more awkward between Jason and me, no matter how much I put into our relationship. I knew I had felt that I was in love with him, and I knew that we were supposed to be engaged, but it sure didn't feel like it anymore. I found myself trying to remember the way I had felt in New Zealand the day he proposed. Our connection didn't feel as real as it had there. One main reason for this was that I couldn't talk to anyone about it. I had to come home, resume my normal life, and pretend that this journey had never happened—and that took a lot of the emotion out of the whole thing. It was a struggle to keep this wonderful secret to myself. Who doesn't want to tell the world they're in love? Even more, when they're engaged? I sure did. But instead I was sneaking outside to talk to Jason on the phone while I was at work, for fear that someone would catch on to who was on the other end of the line. It was hard.

Now, keep in mind, this is all my side of the story, and it's how *I* felt things happened. I had noticed that Jason seemed to be the first one to pull back from the relationship. I didn't feel like he was as excited to talk to me on the phone as he had been. He didn't respond to as many of my text messages or emails as he once had. He just didn't seem to be as interested in me as he had been only a few weeks before.

So, still trying to keep the relationship alive, I sent Hanukkah presents to Jason's son, hoping that the gesture would make us feel like a family. Even though we were two thousand miles apart, I wanted to show that I was thinking about him and his family. The strange thing was, I didn't even get a verbal thank you or just a quick mention that he had received them, let alone any indication that his son had liked them. This really upset me because I had put a lot of thought into trying to figure out what he would really like. It reminded me of a relationship pattern I was used to: Put effort in. Get nothing back.

Unfortunately, we were not strong enough as a couple for me to talk to Jason about what I was feeling. And so, again, I didn't say anything.

Hello, old cycle.

Even though my feelings were hurt, I wasn't giving up. I spent a lot of time trying to figure out why Jason and I weren't working. Maybe it was the age difference, or maybe it was just that we were at different places in our lives. He'd been married. He'd been divorced. He's got a kid. He lives in Seattle. We don't get to see each other. We still haven't gotten to be a real couple yet. We went from an on-camera relationship to living in different states.

I tried to evaluate all the possible explanations for what was wrong, and, ultimately, I think we just didn't mesh. Our personalities and interests were completely different. I'm not sure we were looking for the same things in our lives.

The problem was that we hadn't known how different we were before we got engaged. And I was still very serious about trying to make our engagement work. I even sat down and made a list, more than once, that read, "What do I love about him?"

The only thing I could think to write down was that he was a good dad. And he *was* a good dad, but that wasn't enough reason to be in love with somebody. I truly believe that when there's no connection, it can't be forced. But, even though all signs were pointing toward disaster, I was still holding on to Jason.

I had tried to return to some kind of a normal routine in Dallas. But it was difficult, because my mind was so consumed. I moved into a new apartment with another one of my girlfriends. I returned to my cube at the liquor distribution company. I definitely wasn't a much better employee than I had been when my heart was broken over Tye.

Only this time, I had two people to think about at work. I was back to thinking about Tye again, just because of his constant attempts to get in touch with me. And now I was thinking about Jason, too. My office phone would ring, and it would be Jason; we often had our daily phone calls while I was at work. A song would come on the radio, and it would remind me of Tye because it was one we had listened to together.

Boy, this back-to-reality thing was harder than I thought.

After Jason and I had been home for a few weeks, and around the time that our communication was really starting to fall off, *The Bachelor* press tour started. This meant that Jason was doing the talk-show circuit to promote the first episode, which was scheduled to air on January 5, 2009. Suddenly he had something to talk about, and that's all he would talk to me about. It was slightly irritating, considering that we'd had nothing to talk about before the press tour. Now I just oohed and aahed over the people he was going to meet and the things he was going to do. I wasn't impressed by things like that, and I didn't think he was either, from what he'd told me. But it seemed like he was.

I didn't want to hear about how he had been on *Ellen.* And how he was going to do *Jimmy Kimmel* next, and go out on the town with a bunch of producers afterward. I wanted something deeper than that in terms of the communication I was having with my future husband. I suddenly felt (and no disrespect to Jason here, but it's how I felt at the time) that the press and celebrity were more important to him than I was.

I got it. In that moment, he *was* a big deal. He had a good three weeks of promotion, during which the whole world seemed to be all about him. He was everywhere. He was on magazine covers. He was on talk shows. He was all over the Internet.

All of this might have been fine, or at least easier for me to handle, if he had mixed in any questions about what was going on with me. Or how I was dealing with all of the press. Of course, our engagement was still a secret. And so, in all of these interviews that he was giving, he was talking about how great the other girls were, and how difficult it had been to decide at the end. I knew that, contractually, he was not allowed to say anything other than that. And that he was probably just trying to get people excited for the show. But he had no empathy for what it was like for me to have to hear all of that come out of his mouth. Especially when he talked, during interviews, about that final day, and how the decision was just absolutely grueling for him to make.

Awesome. Just what I want to hear from my fiancé. He was torn over the decision between marrying me or someone else five minutes before he put a ring on my finger.

The fact that I had no one (no friends, and no Jason) to talk to about all of my emotions during this time made me feel completely overwhelmed. How was I supposed to deal with all of that by myself? Not to mention what was in the background, but still very much present, during all of this: Tye.

Jason's interests had definitely turned from the two of us, and our relationship, to himself and his fame. At least, that's how I felt. I found myself wondering, *Is he the person who I want to be with?*

As much as I had fallen in love with him and felt committed to making it work because I had accepted his proposal, I knew that I didn't want to be with someone who was consumed by the entertainment world. Maybe that was just his way of taking the focus away from our cracked relationship—if he consumed himself with his new world, he wouldn't have to deal with the fact that things between us were anything but perfect—but it still hurt me a great deal to watch him do it.

Because I was trying to be supportive and save our relationship, I felt like I had to act super-interested in all of the talk-show and magazine stuff that he was telling me about. Meanwhile, the rest of our conversations had ground to a halt. I still didn't really even know what he did for a living. Insurance, something—I think?

I had no idea about even the basics of his real day-to-day life beyond *The Bachelor*. We had never talked about our relationship and what was going to happen now that the show was over. We never talked about when we were getting married, and if I was moving to Seattle. It got to the point where, if I saw he was calling, I didn't necessarily want to pick up my phone. (That's a terrible way to feel toward your supposed fiancé, don't you think?!)

My day was over earlier than his because of the time difference between Dallas and Seattle, and so I'd sit there with my phone in my hand, take a deep breath, and basically force myself to call him. When I did, I was back to planning out things to say to him again, just so we'd have something to talk about, while I kept my fingers crossed that his voicemail would pick up. I almost felt like I had to talk to him on the phone because, heck, I was engaged to him. But more and more it felt like I was forcing myself to have a relationship with a stranger. Obviously, those were all huge red flags that something was seriously wrong, and I had no idea what to do about it. But I really thought that once the show was done airing, and we could really be together, that we'd be all right again.

The week before Christmas, after I'd been home from the show for about three weeks, my friend Jen and I went to see the Dallas Mavericks basketball team play a home game. It was a Wednesday night, so there weren't that many people out. And we shouldn't really have gone out afterward, since we had work the next day, but we didn't feel like going straight home. We chose this little dive bar near the American Airlines Center to grab a late-night bite. When we walked in, there were maybe ten people in the room, and one of them happened to be Tye, who was out with his friends. This was the first time I had seen him since our "final conversation."

Not that long before this moment, my heart would have leapt into my throat if I saw him. I would have analyzed his every word and look for any sign of interest or affection. But I was a new woman now. I was engaged, and even though Jason and I hadn't seen each other since the show ended, and were talking less and less, I was still committed to making our relationship work. I had really moved on.

I walked right up to Tye. I felt confident, and good, and very strong.

"Hi there," I said.

We caught up a little bit, just small talk, and that was it. In my mind, I had gotten to this new place where I thought we could really just be friends. It was a relief, actually, to look at him as a friend instead of thinking, *Please, please, ask me out tomorrow night. Let's go to a movie. I'll do anything for us to be together.*

I was continuing to withhold all information about anything that had happened on the show. Not only because I was contractually obligated to keep quiet, but because I didn't feel like I owed him anything.

At one point in the night, I walked outside to talk to Jason on the phone, and Jen came out with me. Weirdly, Tye followed us out of the bar onto the sidewalk. I couldn't figure out what he was doing. I wanted to keep talking to Jason without Tye overhearing me, so I basically started running down the street away from him to have some privacy.

And then, good friend that she is, Jen got in between Tye and me. "Stay here," she ordered him. "Stay here."

Apparently that's not all she said, either. Jen lit into Tye, letting him know just how badly he had treated me, and how low her opinion of him was because of it.

Gotta love great friends!

When I finally said good night to Jason and went back into the bar, Jen and I sat down together at a table, talking. We had our phones out in front of us, like people always do, just in case someone called or texted us. Tye and his friends were at another table nearby.

I got up to go to the bathroom. Jen turned away from our table for a minute to talk to someone else. When she turned back, one of Tye's friends had snuck up to our table. He had her cell phone in his hand.

"What are you doing with my phone?" Jen asked angrily.

He looked at her sheepishly, made an excuse, and dropped her phone back onto our table. Then, he hurried back to where Tye and his friends were sitting. I didn't learn any of this until later, but apparently, Tye and his friends were dying to know if I actually was with Jason or not. They figured that if they found Jason's number in my phone, they would know we were talking and, therefore, were engaged. So Tye's friend had volunteered to play detective. Just not very well. *Nicely done, MacGyver.*

I'm sure I would have been flattered if I had known about this, but it wouldn't have really mattered. I was still happily wrapped up in my little wonderland where I was engaged and in love. I do have to admit, though, it was weird seeing Tye that night. Even though I was in a new place in my life, I couldn't deny that there was something there between the two of us. But I just figured that when you've loved someone so much for so long, there will always be a part of you that won't let go 100 percent. I didn't think any further about it.

That night, when Jen was driving us home, Tye kept calling my phone. I kept letting it go to voicemail. Finally, at one point, she got fed up. She snatched my phone from me.

"Let me answer it," she said.

I laughed, thinking, *Oh,* this *should be good!*

"What?" she snapped.

"Where are you guys going?" he asked.

"We're going home, Tye," she said. "It's late."

And she hung up.

That was just the start of it. He called back again. This time I answered.

"Dude, what?" I said. "I just saw you."

"I just wanted to say, 'Be careful on your way home,'" he said.

The guy was relentless. He really was.

"We will be," I said. "Good night."

I hung up the phone and turned to Jen, who was looking at me.

"What?" I asked.

She just shook her head.

After that night, Tye continued to pursue me. He would call, text, and email me throughout the day, sometimes just saying hello, and sometimes asking me to go somewhere or do something with him. My typical response was no. I have to admit that it felt really good to be getting this attention from someone I had so desperately wanted it from for so long. But I just didn't respond to it the way I would have a year earlier. As good as it felt, I had no intentions of going down that road again.

But once things started really going bad with Jason, and Tye continued to call, I have to admit that I was tempted. I figured that one dinner couldn't hurt. And then, once I had decided to go out with him, I started to look forward to it. I had some things to get off my chest (again!).

One of the many times Tye called and asked me to go to dinner, I finally accepted. I think he was shocked.

There was a stipulation, however: "We can go to dinner, but only as friends," I clarified.

That's exactly what we did. Or *I* did. I was in this other place. I was with somebody else. I had moved on, and even if it was a struggle to keep my relationship with Jason going at that point, I certainly wasn't interested in restarting a relationship with Tye again. It literally felt like he was just my friend, nothing more. We talked like buddies over dinner.

"What's been going on?" I said. "How's the agency coming?"

Not only that, but I actually felt confident enough to ask him about his personal life.

"Are you dating anybody?" I asked. "Have you seen anybody since, you know, a couple of months ago?"

We had a nice time, laughed a lot, and caught up some. And then, at the end of dinner, he showed me that he wasn't quite as ready to just be friends as I was.

He walked me out to my car just like a gentleman. But when I turned around to hug him good-bye, he had this look on his face.

Oh gosh, I've seen that look! Don't do it, Tye. Don't do it!

But he did. He leaned down and tried to kiss me. I turned my head and backed away from him.

"Don't," I whispered.

"Why not?" Tye asked. He was not used to being rejected.

"Because, Tye!" I said. "We've been down this path before, and it doesn't work."

He had made this awkward now. I turned, got in my car, and drove away.

On my way home, I called Jason. I told him I'd had dinner with a friend, which in my mind was the absolute truth, because Tye was nothing more than a friend to me at that point. We talked the entire way home, just doing the typical couple thing of checking in about how each of our days had been.

Literally, every two minutes, Tye kept calling in. Every time I saw his name come up on my phone, I wondered why he wouldn't stop, especially after the way we'd just left things.

When I got home, I was still talking to Jason. We talked for maybe two hours. When we hung up, I finally called Tye back.

"What's the deal?" I demanded.

"Well, why didn't you pick up when I called?" he said. "Where were you?"

"Tye, what are you talking about?" I said. "I was busy. Why would I have picked up your phone call? I just saw you."

"Were you talking to somebody else?" he said.

Are you kidding me?

"Tye, I'm not going to talk to you about this," I said.

I think it finally clicked in his mind. I didn't have to tell him I was involved with someone else. At this point, he had figured it out. And it had to have stung. I don't think he thought I would really move on. Heck, I hadn't thought I would ever really move on.

But as satisfying as it felt to know that Tye was aware that I had moved on, after everything he had put me through, I was still emotionally conflicted. I had been so happy with Tye and then had gotten my heart broken. And then I had been so happy with Jason, but things just felt odd between us. Why did it seem like, every time I truly felt happy, history seemed to repeat itself and leave me in the lurch once again?

nine

"STRICKTLY"
PLATONIC

Having to internalize everything that I was going through was near impossible. I wasn't any more captivated by my job than I had previously been, and so I had nothing to distract me from thinking about my romantic problems, constantly, at work during the day. I thought about them at night, too, because I didn't have the Cowboys to distract me anymore. And, yes, I thought about them in the mornings. And on weekends. In fact, there wasn't a time when I was not thinking about them.

At least, for once, I hadn't been afraid to tell Tye what I needed from him, which was for him to leave me alone. Not that it was easy to do so. It took a lot. But it also felt good. I could tell, even then, that it was a very defining time for me, and that I was gaining a lot of independence. I felt like I was in control for once. I was grabbing ahold of the reigns and actually thinking about what I wanted to do with my life.

On the one hand, if I stuck with the decision I had made, I'd be in Seattle. I'd be a stepmom, which would mean getting a start on the family that was so important to me. I'd be with a man who had made me feel beautiful and intelligent and funny, and who had given me the confidence to get back on my feet after the worst period of my entire life, and who had—up until now—made me feel so special. But my husband would potentially be somebody who really wanted the spotlight.

On the other hand, if I took this other road, and I went with Tye, I'd be going with the guy who had always made me happier, always made me laugh more, and who still always gave me that same old feeling of *"It's Tye, it's always been Tye."* But, even more important, I was afraid that I couldn't trust him. If I did, I knew there was a chance that I could end up exactly where I had been a few months before. Because, as dense as I had been about Tye, and as much as I had lived in denial about the way he treated me, once I went on *The Bachelor,* I finally got clear on the message Tye had been trying to give me for months before: He didn't want me. He had ignored me, disrespected me, done whatever he wanted, even when it made me cry (even though I had never let him know he made me cry). So now it was hard to believe that he thought a few text messages were enough to show that his feelings and intentions had changed, just like that.

It was an internal battle. And because it was occupying so much of my thoughts, I often didn't want to talk to anybody. I didn't want to talk to Tye and have him try to win me over. I didn't want to talk to Jason and have him *not* try to win me over, or not even do or say the smallest thing to make me feel closer to him and believe our future together.

I think the worst part was that I couldn't really talk to anybody about what was going on, and so I had to stuff so much down deep inside. Almost nobody knew I was engaged. My parents knew, but I was not about to tell them about the turmoil that was going on in my life. Tye knew something was up, but I certainly wasn't at a point where I was talking to him about any of this stuff. Nobody knew what Jason and I were going through, or that it seemed increasingly likely that we would break up. Nobody knew that Tye was trying to come back into my life.

It was all on me to figure everything out on my own. And I don't know if a person can do that rationally. Having nobody to talk to made me suddenly realize how much we all need a friend to be a sounding board, just to sit there so we can say, "I have got to tell you what is going on in my life right now."

And so the friend can say, "Listen, you've got these heart goggles on, and this is clearly a really bad decision."

Or

"I know he's pulling back, but you need to stick with it."

Or

"Give Tye another chance."

I had none of that.

Then, on January 3, 2009, Tye called me while I was heading to my friend Robin's house for dinner. I didn't always answer when he called, but for some reason, this time I picked up.

After making our usual small talk, Tye dropped an emotional bomb on me.

"Melissa, I know I can't give you an explanation as to why now," he said. "I don't know. I just know that I have never been surer of anything in my life than I am that I want to be with you. I do love you. And I know, as dumb as this sounds right now, I know that I'm going to marry you."

Instead of making me giddy with happiness like it would have done the year before, I didn't want to hear it. As far as I was concerned, it was too little, too late. I was still convinced that he wanted me only because I had told him that he couldn't have me, and that he wanted me even more now that he knew he *really* couldn't have me.

"Tye, I can't do this," I said. "Listen, I need you to be my friend right now. And if you can't talk to me like a friend and treat me like a friend, then you need to stop calling me. You need to leave me alone."

"Tell me there's a glimmer of hope that we might get back together, and I'm going to stay," Tye said. "But if you tell me to move on, I'm going to move on."

I sat there for what felt like a long time.

Just say it. Say it!

I thought about it, and then shrugged my shoulders.

"You need to move on," I said. "You need to go and move on with your life, because we are never going to be together."

He didn't say anything at first. Maybe he was shocked. Maybe he felt weird about being rejected. I don't know. But then, he just started shouting.

"No, no I don't!" He was literally screaming into the phone. "We were meant to be together, and I know that!"

It was strange hearing him like this. Tye was always so put together, calm, and rational. And this kind of behavior was something I had never seen from him.

"Tye, you asked me to tell you something, and I told it to you," I said. "It's just not what you wanted to hear." I felt bad, I really did. But what could I do?

"Tye, I really can't do this right now, okay?" I said.

And with that, I hung up.

What the heck had just happened? I couldn't believe he'd just said that to me!

What I didn't know until later was that ever since I had gotten back to Dallas from *The Bachelor,* Tye had prayed, and prayed, and prayed about our relationship, and when he woke up that morning (he's always remembered that it was January 3, which is the only reason I know that date!), it had come to him that he would marry me someday. He could never tell me why or how he knew. He just did.

What I also learned later was that he called his sister that night. Tye and his sister were very close, so he was going to her for advice. He told her that he was going to go to my apartment, flowers in hand, and tell me exactly how he felt about me, and that he was going to fight to get me back.

She gave him some pretty good advice. "Don't get in the way of her relationship," his sister said. "She's happy now. She's in a good place. Unless you are prepared to say you love her and want to marry her, and actually mean it, then leave her alone and let her move on."

That night, Tye actually did show up at my apartment with a bouquet of flowers. So much for listening to sisterly advice!

Only, I wasn't home, I was out to dinner with my friend Robin. When he realized that I wasn't at home, he called me.

"Please come home," he said. "I'm at your door."

This was a whole new side of Tye that I had never seen before. And it would have been sweet. Except! He had only been to my apartment once before, in the year and a half that we had dated, and only then because I had really needed him to help me move my belongings in. And so, again, this was too little, too late.

"Tye, I'm out to dinner," I said. "I'm not going to be home for a while. Leave my house."

"No," he said. "I need to talk to you." Oh my gosh, he was stubborn!

"Listen," I said. "If you leave my house right now, I will stop by later, and I will give you five minutes to say whatever you need to say. Five minutes."

I didn't feel like I owed him anything more than that at this point. I had said everything I needed to say, and I continued to be convinced that he just wanted me back because he had missed me while I was gone, and now that I was back, he couldn't have me. And he had probably gotten flack from all of his friends about the fact that he had lost me to *The Bachelor*.

When I got over to Tye's house that night, his roommate was home, and so we went out to the garage and sat in his car, just to have some privacy. He wanted to talk. I sat there staring at him and wondering what he could possibly have left to say.

Even when he first started talking, it wasn't immediately clear what he was trying to tell me. Everything he said came out wrong.

"I'm sorry I didn't like you a whole lot before," he said.

I just looked at him. *Way to make a girl feel special, Tye.*

"No, that's not what I meant," he said.

He was nervous.

"You were always the one, but you weren't the only one," he said.

"What?" I looked at him in disbelief. *Wow, you really are bad at this!*

"No, wait!" he said. "That's not what I meant."

He got quiet for a long moment, like he was gathering his strength.

"Melissa, you cannot tell me that you have more fun with this guy than with me," he said. "Or that you love him more than you love me."

He looked so sweet and serious. And this wasn't just some guy. This was Tye. He was telling me everything that I had always wanted to hear from him. I wanted to believe him, but he had hurt me so badly. I couldn't help myself: I started to cry. Too many emotions were running through me. I'd finally hit emotional overload.

"Maybe," I said. "But he doesn't make me cry like you did. And I know he won't hurt me like you did."

Tye lost it at that point. He was crying harder than I was. I just looked at him.

"You sit here and say that you want me, you want me, you want me," I said. "Why didn't you want me four months ago? What happened between now and then?"

"I don't know," he said. "I can't tell you what happened."

"Well, I don't believe you," I said. "I think you want me because you can't have me right now. And that's not fair. You took me for granted. Do you know how much I did for you? And how much of my time I spent making you crap and buying you dinner? And you didn't even seem to notice it until I was gone."

It was like the night we broke up, and once I got started, I couldn't stop. "You probably noticed I was gone only because you didn't have Starbucks in the morning," I said. "Or you had to go a football season without having cookies there to eat. I mean, that's the only way you knew I was around, isn't it?"

Tye didn't even try to defend himself. He was a mess. He just looked miserable.

"I am making myself sick thinking about you," he said. "I have never felt this way about anyone before. I love you so much. I've never said that to any girl, other than my sister and my mom."

He was crying so hard, he was literally going through tissues by the second.

"I can't go out anymore," he said. "At night, my friends go out, and I literally sit at home by myself. I can't do anything. I can't function. I'm miserable."

I did start to feel bad then. I knew that feeling Tye was describing, and I wouldn't have wished it upon my worst enemy. It was heartbreaking. But, I'll be honest, there was also a part of me that was glad that he was finally feeling an ounce of what I had felt for a year and a half.

Good, I'm glad you feel like that because you take that times a million, times six months, and that's exactly what I felt like.

But I didn't want him to hurt. I don't think any of us ever wants anybody we love to hurt. He had never felt like that before. He had never had something that he wanted be unreachable. He had never had a girl tell him no. And I was glad that he finally knew what heartbreak felt like. Maybe this would make him more sympathetic and not just take the next girl who came along for granted.

"I love you," he said. "I know I took you for granted. And it kills me to see how much I've hurt you. And I can't live without you."

I sat in his passenger seat, trying to absorb everything that he was saying to me. As much as I loved hearing what he said, I couldn't do anything about it now. I was in another place and couldn't disrespect my new relationship by responding to him.

"Tye, my loyalty's not with you anymore," I said. "You're not my priority anymore."

He looked like I had just punched him in the face, and it broke a piece of my heart. As much, and as badly, as he had hurt me, I hated hurting him. I heard once that true love is when just the thought of hurting the person you love hurts you more. Three years later, I can now see why it bothered me so much to watch him hurt over me, but at the time, I was too confused to understand everything I was feeling.

Here I was, turning down the love of my life while defending a guy who I wasn't even technically really involved with anymore. But I had put so much into trying to make it work with Jason that I couldn't just give up like that. And I couldn't just trust Tye, either. Not after everything he had done—and failed to do.

I couldn't believe what I was hearing come out of Tye's mouth, but I couldn't take it, either. We left things unfinished that night. There was no closure to the conversation. But I knew I needed to get out. Ironically, I just needed to talk to Jason about what was happening. So I called him on my way home—and he never answered. The one person's voice that I needed to hear right then, and he didn't pick up.

The next day while I was at work, Tye sent me a huge email. I almost couldn't deal with it on top of everything else. I had one relationship completely crumbling from beneath me. I felt like I had no control over it, and I was starting to wonder if I wanted control over it, or even any part of it. And then, I had this guy—*the guy*—coming back, making more of an effort in five days than I had ever seen him make in the years that I had known him.

In his email, Tye described how he had reevaluated his life and recommitted himself to his faith in order to start living a better life and be a better man. He took responsibility for all of the ways he had hurt and disappointed me in the past. He reiterated how much he loved me and wanted to be with me. And he resolved to win me over in the future.

"I am honoring your request for time to think about and deal with things. I will be waiting for you. I want you. I need you. And I love you. Also, I am copying my family on this email. I want them to know how I feel as well. I hope this is okay, but for the first time in a long time, I am actually *proud* of a decision that I am making."

I looked at the cc: line to see that his whole family actually was copied on the email. *Wow. He was serious.*

Though the words and the sentiment were beautiful, given everything I was going through, it just felt like more pressure. So I wrote back and basically said, "You have to respect the situation that I'm in. I know we're not talking about it, and I know we're not able to be open about it, but you have to respect that I'm in another relationship. And I'm really trying to make it work. It may not work, and I don't think it's going to work. But you have to at least give me that chance to sort these feelings out on my own. I don't want you to sway me. I don't want you sitting in front of me telling me something that's going to make me think differently about the situation. If you cannot be my friend, if you cannot talk to me like a friend, you cannot talk to me right now. From here on out, until I tell you otherwise, our relationship is strictly platonic. I just need some time. You need to respect my time right now."

I did need time. I was in a hot mess of an emotional state. I really was. I was trying to figure out this crazy point in my life, but all I had were questions without answers: *Why was I put in this situation? How did it get this far with Jason?* I kept going over and over it in my mind, and I didn't have any idea how to make sense of it all. It was like I was at war with myself. I kept battling myself over what I knew rather than what I felt. I wanted to do what was right. But I didn't know how, or even what that was.

I was in this pickle of a situation, and it just wasn't working. But I felt like I had to make it work, even if I had lost sight of why. I had a ring. I'd made this commitment. Clearly, I had thought I was in love with Jason. Maybe I still was. And I was just going through withdrawal, and I just needed to see him again to make things right.

Or maybe I had just made the biggest mistake of my entire life.

And was about to go through the most embarrassing experience of my entire life. Everyone I knew had seen me come home so blissed out, and everybody in America was about to see me being so happy and in love on the show. But things were falling apart, and it looked like Jason and I could very well end up being a statistic.

On the other hand, for some reason that I still couldn't understand, I now had this other person, Tye, who was like this fly right in front of my face that just wouldn't go away, even when I shooed it. And I was avidly trying to shoo it away.

I had asked Tye to respect the situation I was in. And he did. He didn't call me or text me after he got my email. Soon after that, though, I was at work one morning when the receptionist called me to her desk, giddy with excitement. When I walked up, there was a flower arrangement sitting there. I looked at the beautiful colors and drew a blank. I really didn't have any idea who could have sent me flowers. I knew it could have been one of two people, but neither of them seemed likely. Tye had never, ever sent me flowers during the eighteen months we had dated. And Jason and I were not on very good terms at this point. I thought that, maybe, he had sent me flowers to try to make up for everything. But I kind of doubted that he would do that, and so I really had no idea.

I opened up the card, and all it said was "Stricktly Platonic."

Tye's last name is Strickland. I saw the spelling of *Stricktly* and figured out that they were from Tye. *Very clever, Strickland.*

I couldn't believe it. These were the very first flowers he had ever sent me. They sat in my cube for days, and all the while, I couldn't decide what to say to Tye about them. And so I became the kind of person I had always been mad at Tye for being when we first dated. I didn't contact him. I didn't thank him. That's so not me, but I couldn't bring myself to do anything because I had no idea what was happening with Jason or how I felt about it. But I kept the flowers and dried them out—and I still have them to this day.

I wasn't ready to let Tye back in. Meanwhile, Jason and I were barely talking anymore. We'd never had a fight or a disagreement. It had just sort of faded away. And to be honest, I was irritated that he hadn't made more of an effort to make this relationship work. I felt like I had actually tried, and he seemed to have given up.

On top of that, I had actually heard something disturbing about Jason from one of the girlfriends I had stayed in touch with since *The Bachelor*. She told me that Molly had called her and told her that she and Jason were talking.

I called Jason immediately to see if it was true. "I have to ask you something," I said.

"Sure."

"I heard from one of the other girls that you and Molly have been talking," I said.

"No, we haven't," he replied. "I called her a while ago to check on her and make sure that she was okay. But that's it."

I don't know that I entirely believed him, but maybe I was at the point where I didn't care enough to push for the truth, even if I couldn't admit it to myself yet. It kind of got to the point where I almost didn't want to talk to him because I didn't have anything to say. And I'm sure he didn't have anything to say to me, either. Sometimes when we did talk, he would let his son, Ty, get on the phone with me. He's such a sweet kid, and I really enjoyed that, especially since it had gotten so awkward between Jason and I. But looking back, I wish Jason hadn't done this, because I feel like it could have only been confusing for Ty. As time went on, it was increasingly hard for me to imagine the three of us ever being the family I had once hoped we would be.

I finally got frustrated with Jason, maybe because the more Tye persisted, the more the possibility of a relationship with my ex started to look better and better. And the differences between Jason and I were blaringly obvious at this point.

I'm not going to get too specific on all the details of the demise of our relationship, but I do remember at one point distinctly asking if his feelings had changed. And if he was thinking about getting in touch with Molly. And he said no.

But I didn't really believe him. We never talked about the wedding. We never talked about anything in the future, other than me potentially moving to Seattle, and even that had been mentioned maybe only one or two times right in the beginning. We didn't say "I love you" on the phone. We didn't call each other "babe" or any of the sweet little terms of endearment we'd had for each other. It was literally like two friends talking on the phone. And not even good friends. But neither of us said anything about it. And neither of us asked if we should call it quits.

We just stopped talking altogether.

ten

AFTER THE
FINAL ROSE

n the middle of all this confusion in my personal life, the thirteenth season of *The Bachelor* began airing. I hadn't been able to tell anyone about the turmoil I had been going through since I got back to Dallas. By the time the show was about to air, ABC had already announced the cast of *The Bachelor* Season 13. So everyone soon found out the answer to where I had been for the last several months. My name, picture, and bio were plastered all over *The Bachelor* website. And all around me, people wanted to know everything about what happened on the show. Nothing had aired yet, and no one had any clue what actually did happen. Slightly overwhelming . . .

I had decided that I didn't want to watch the show. Jason and I were still "together" (maybe not on the best of terms, but still technically together), and I didn't want to have to see him with all of the other girls on the show. I knew I would be exposed to things I hadn't seen while I was there: the dates he went on, the kisses he had shared with the other girls, the feelings he developed for some of the girls. And I just didn't want to see it.

But of course, my friends proposed that we have *Bachelor*-watching parties. I mean, it sounds like a great idea. I would love to watch one of my friends on TV, but this felt weird. I suddenly realized, they were all going to watch me try and *date* . . . and honestly, that's a little awkward.

"Why wouldn't you want to watch it?" they asked. "We thought this was going to be a good thing. You seemed so happy when you came home!"

I didn't feel like having to explain why I was so against it, so I gave in and compromised. I decided I'd just watch the first episode. *Nothing could have happened in the first episode that would upset me, right? Right.*

When my girlfriends saw me on TV, they cheered and laughed. They couldn't understand why I wasn't more pumped up about the experience. I felt so uncomfortable watching myself. I was suddenly seeing things I'd never seen before.

Hmmm . . . I walk kinda funny . . .

I didn't know my voice was quite that annoying. . . .

I cringed watching myself. And knowing what was going to happen, both on the show and in its aftermath, made watching the show even worse. Not only that, but when I saw myself on the show, it felt like I was watching some other girl who wasn't me. I looked so young and naïve. All right folks, I get that it had happened only four months earlier . . . but I just looked like a lost little girl to me. Only a handful of people knew what I was going through right before *The Bachelor* started taping, and although I think I hid it from most people, looking back . . . I could see that lost girl.

During the show's airing was a really hard time for me. I was in this weird limbo, where Jason and I weren't really talking anymore, and Tye and I weren't really talking, either. And so, everything in my life felt shaky and uncertain. Especially me. Why did everything seem to be so difficult? The emotional cycle just *would not end.*

I can't even accurately describe the emotional stress that I was going through at the time the show was actually airing. Let's recap: I had been madly in love with Tye in Dallas; gotten my heart completely shattered by Tye; then he kind of decided he wanted me back . . . but only occasionally; I went on *The Bachelor* journey looking for a new direction for my life; I met Jason and fell for him; I got *engaged* to him; Tye decided that he wanted me back, permanently, but I was finally in a place where I was angry at him and didn't want to talk to him; my relationship with Jason was a struggle; I was in limbo with my relationship to both Tye and Jason. And oh yeah, add the fact that I couldn't talk to anyone about what I was dealing with, and that's just about the perfect recipe for an emotional disaster.

Little did I know, that the next event that took place in my life would be the most life-changing incident ever. We had finished filming *The Bachelor* for about three months, and now it was time to film the "After the Final Rose" special. I was dreading having to face that situation. A huge part of me was humiliated that I had gotten so wrapped up in the process, and another part of me was humiliated that we were going to have to admit that we were not as happy and in love as we looked when we got engaged.

Are we supposed to talk about how great things were between us? Or are we supposed to be honest and say that things had become very awkward? Would we decide to make it work? Or would we decide to part ways?

It's really sad that Jason and I weren't even really talking by this point. We had a few phone conversations about filming the "After" special, but nothing really substantial. I definitely felt uncomfortable. He and I were long past pretending that we were so in love and happy, or even still engaged. We both knew that we weren't really together, and I didn't expect that we were going to pretend that we were a couple for the cameras. But there had been no official end, either. Neither one of us had actually suggested that we should just cut the ties and make a public announcement, or at least start telling anybody who asked us that we weren't together anymore. So I had no idea what our actual status was.

The night before I flew to Los Angeles to tape "After the Final Rose," Tye invited me over for dinner. When I got to his condo, it was clear that he had planned a date-type evening for us. It was almost an exact repeat of the night we had together, right before I left for *The Bachelor.* Again, he had even gotten takeout from my favorite restaurant, Sushi Zushi. But he had put a lot more thought into making this night special than he had ever done before. When I saw that he had my favorite rolls, I looked at him and thought, *I didn't even know you knew what my favorite stuff was.*

We went upstairs to the roof and had a nice conversation while we ate. It wasn't exactly romantic, which I think was better for me, given everything else I had going on at the time. Really, Tye and I were just enjoying the feeling of reconnecting as we talked. And there was a lot to catch up on. I'd missed two months of life in Dallas while I was on *The Bachelor,* and so we went over everything he and his buddies had been up to, and his family, and my family. In some ways, the conversation was pretty on the surface. But it was always more than that with us. And it was such a relief to talk so easily after all of the awkwardness during my phone calls with Jason. Tye and I never ran out of stuff to say. It was always one thing after another with us, with lots of laughing and jokes. I felt like I had my buddy back, but better.

I was impressed by how much care Tye had put into the night. And I could tell that he was listening to me and taking note of things I said in a way that he never had done before. At the end of dinner, he didn't want me to go home. Things definitely felt different than they had before. The power had shifted, and I wasn't this scared little girl begging for his affection anymore. He wanted me there. That night, he became my confidant. Someone I could finally talk to about everything I had been going through and feeling. It sounds odd that the person I ended up confiding in was someone I had once been so in love with, but it just felt so natural and easy to talk to him. That's when I decided to start letting him in on what was going on with *The Bachelor.*

"I have to go film this 'After the Final Rose' thing soon," I said.

"I don't want you to go do that," he said. He actually looked nervous.

Maybe he didn't want me to leave him again. Maybe he just didn't want me to see Jason, out of fear that it would rekindle the feelings that we had felt. I don't know. It was just a small moment, and not enough to give me real clarity or comfort during a time when both of the major relationships in my life were in such a weird place. But it felt good to hear him say that he wanted me to stay, since it had been him telling me to go that had originally set this whole crazy odyssey in motion.

I remember thinking that night how I felt just being with Tye . . . not dating him, not wooing him, but just sitting and talking with him. And it felt great. It was a feeling I had never experienced with Jason. And to be frank, I didn't even get to experience it with Tye when we had dated previously. He had never really let me into the place that he did that night on his roof. We were both vulnerable, and leaning on each other, and enjoying our *friendship* for really the first time.

The next day, I took off for Los Angeles to face the dreaded "After the Final Rose" taping. I was getting very anxious just sitting on the plane. I was about to face people who I hadn't seen in months . . . most important the man who I was *engaged* to but had such an awkward relationship with. I had no idea what was about to happen, or what we were going to do. And the fact that my communication with Jason had basically ceased, I wasn't getting much direction from him.

I began replaying the entire experience in my head. What I felt when I first saw Jason . . . reliving our first date . . . remembering our proposal. How would I feel when I saw him? Would it make me remember how I felt on the show? Would I get angry as to how things turned out? Would I be able to confront Jason about why he didn't at least try to make this work? Did I even care?

So many questions were swirling in my head, and I just had a huge pit in my stomach. And it was so weird that Jason and I hadn't talked *at all* about what we were going to do or say. The more I thought about it, the angrier I got. *Why hadn't Jason talked to me before we came here to film this? Aren't I at least owed that? I mean, he friggin'* proposed *to me!* And here I was, having to face him after months, and talk about our relationship in front of the camera. I didn't want to talk about what was going on, or wrong, in our relationship with cameras rolling. I felt they were conversations that needed to take place privately first.

I was sitting backstage, just about to walk on the stage with Jason and host Chris Harrison, and I had all of these emotions bottled up inside of me, which was the perfect combustible material for good TV. One wrong word was going to make all of my feelings come pouring out in a way that I was afraid I was going to regret later.

To start off the segment, they showed the footage from the day we got engaged in New Zealand. Now, keep in mind, the show was still airing at this time, so none of us had seen the proposal—neither I nor Jason. And watching it made me tear up. And I'll be honest, I don't know why. Part was sadness, part was embarrassment. . . . I was definitely overwhelmed, and the emotional ride I'd been on felt like it was about to explode.

I awkwardly walked out on stage . . . I didn't even know whether I should hug Jason or not. And I was so upset that this was now going to be discussed publicly, that I was literally shaking. Chris set Jason up to start talking, and Jason launched into this big speech about how he'd wanted to give me everything when he proposed to me, but he now felt like things had changed between us.

He fidgeted in his seat while he talked, "I mean, our conversations over the last few weeks have been how things are different . . . How *I* feel like things are different. And we both just watched and saw everything that we've been through. Which every single moment of that experience, for me, was true. I completely fell in love with you . . . I knew on that last day that I wanted to give you everything. I wanted to give you my life, I wanted to give you everything you deserved. But I feel like things are different."

My blood began to boil. *He didn't have the decency to say this to me off camera? He had to wait until I was thrown in front of millions of people?* I could only shake my head in disbelief. I couldn't believe we were having *this* conversation for the first time in front of millions of people!

Jason continued, "I came here to find somebody to spend my life with . . . I . . . We're not right for each other." He stopped, and waited for me to react.

"I don't know what you want me to say when you sit there and say that, because I *don't* believe you." I was literally shaking from anger. Now I was angry that I had just watched this proposal, and heard him say how much he loved me, and wanted to give me everything, and couldn't wait to start a life with me. . . . And now, it's just changed. He had made a commitment to be with me forever. *HE* made the decision to ask me to marry him. *HE* was the one who had been through the experience before, and knew how easy it was to get wrapped up in the process. *HE* was the one who should have known better! And *HE* didn't even want to fight for the relationship. I didn't want him to fight for it now, but he didn't fight for it when it was brand-new . . . when things had started to turn . . . he didn't even try to see if it could work.

I continued on my rant, "I do not see how you can sit there and say what you said to me: 'I love you,' 'I want to spend my life with you,' 'I want to make you happy' . . . and then the second, the *second* you start having doubts, you don't talk to me about it and say 'let's work on this, let's fight. I just put a ring on your finger, so let's see what we can do to fix this.' No, it's 'I'm just gonna pull away. Whoaa, things are different, and I don't even want to try.'" My voice started to shake as I fought back tears. "Do you see where I'm a *little* irritated?"

I glared at him, unable to see anything likeable or good about the man who I had been sure, just a few months ago, was going to be my future husband.

"Of course," he said calmly, "You have every right to be irritated."

"What did I do?" I interrupted him.

He shook his head emphatically. "You didn't do anything."

I totally didn't believe him. How could he decide to propose to me, and then suddenly back away because 'things changed?'

"No, something happened! And you have yet to be honest with me at all, except to say 'I'm sorry.'" I was not going to let him off the hook. He was going to give me some sort of an explanation. 'I'm sorry' was not going to cut it. I stared at him with such anger, until he began his explanation.

"So going back to that final day, what I realized is that I was falling in love with two people at the same time. At the exact same time. And maybe I wasn't the right person to come and do all this, because I didn't think there was any capacity in the world to fall for two people at the same time." He kept looking down when he spoke.

What is he trying to say? That he loved both me and Molly equally? How then, can you make the enormous decision to ask one to marry you, when you are in love with another??

And them—BAM!—out it came! Attacking me like hundreds of knives stabbing my body.

"I still have feelings for Molly."

Well there you go. How could I have been so blind? I was suddenly furious. It all suddenly made total sense to me. Of course he gave up on our relationship. He was starting a new one with someone else. I had tried very hard to make the relationship succeed, when all along he hadn't really put anything into it. So, while I was shopping for his son and sending him funny texts, he was talking to another girl. And once again, I felt like the girl who just wasn't good enough. My stomach started to hurt.

"Have you been talking to her?" I asked angrily.

"No," he answered quickly. Too quickly for my liking. *Well of course. Why would he tell me even if he had been talking to her?*

"I mean, I think the worst thing in the world is to live your life with regrets," he said.

Oh my gosh! Just stop talking already!

"You're such a bastard," I said under my breath. I don't think I've ever been as angry as I was at that moment.

He continued. "And I don't regret anything with you. You are exactly what I was looking for when I came here. And I told you that. And that's the whole truth. But I learned a lot about myself over these past three months."

Umm . . . you mean the three months we were engaged?? You suddenly learned something about yourself? Please continue . . .

"I've grown as a person. There's obviously no way I'm perfect. I mean, look at me."

"Yea, I'll second that . . . I'm sorry," I scoffed.

Jason looked at me. "I don't regret anything that's happened between us. I know you do."

"I do," I snapped back at him. *My turn.* It was finally my chance to speak, and I let it rip.

"I trusted you with everything. To me, getting engaged and finding that person is a once-in-a-lifetime thing. And you took that from me." I tried to continue to fight my tears, but they were coming at this point. "You took it. I wish more than anything that last day, you would have just let me go, instead of doing this to me. I'm so mad at you!"

"I would do anything if I could give that to you," he said.

I held out the ring, and he took it from me. I didn't believe anything he had to say to me anymore. The fact that he couldn't give me some sort of a warning as to what I was walking into had infuriated me. To me, it was unforgivable. Even if he felt he loved Molly, why didn't he just *tell* me that? Excuse me: tell me that *privately*. At least he could have given me a chance to react privately, and get my emotions in check before dealing with it on camera.

"I don't get it at all," I said. "Because none of it makes sense." And in reality, it all did make sense. I was just his second choice.

Just to add salt to my open, bleeding wound, Chris Harrison gave us all a recap of what just happened.

"Just to clarify, you're breaking it off with Melissa, and you're going to pursue a chance—a shot—with Molly." *Thanks, Chris. We needed that clarification.*

"I'm sorry for everything," Jason said.

"You know, I've been through a ton of heartbreak," I said. "You've been through a ton of heartbreak. That's why I'm baffled by all this. I mean, it doesn't make sense. You should know better than to do something like that. So, good luck in the future. Good luck with Molly. There you go. Don't call me. Don't text me anymore. Leave me alone, please. Thank you."

I stood up and stormed off stage. As I walked to the limo waiting for me outside, I went over and over everything in my mind. Every boyfriend I'd ever had, except for Tye, had been unfaithful to me so that was probably my greatest fear when I got into a new relationship. I had actually opened up to Jason enough to tell him this. And he had still gone and done exactly the same thing to me— only he'd done it on national TV. I immediately went back to that place of wondering what was wrong with me that made this always happen to me, and how I could ever trust anyone.

I had not necessarily thought that my relationship with Jason would have worked out anyhow. I was happy with what had developed between Tye and I since Jason and I had fallen apart. But the fact that Jason had given up on us, and gone back to a relationship with another woman immediately after we got engaged, brought back the same old feeling that I'd never *been* enough, and that I would never *be* enough. I was very emotionally fragile right then. And learning that Jason had given in to his feelings for Molly—while I had been putting Tye off out of respect for Jason, and our relationship—broke me.

There was definitely no more Bubble now. And I hated the reality I was facing. All of America—my family, my friends, and Tye—were going to see me be this stupid girl who fell in love in two weeks and then just got absolutely humiliated on national television. My biggest fear, from that day my dad called and told me how nervous he was about what would happen if I went on the show, had come true. And now I was going to have to go home, and everyone was going to laugh at me. Again, I felt like there was no one I could trust. I felt utterly alone, and I was mad that I had gotten myself there.

I'm smarter than this. And I know better. And now I look like that girl. And I don't want to be that girl.

I finally reached the safety of my hotel room and reached out for the best source of comfort I could imagine: I called Tye. He could tell I'd been crying.

"Why are you crying?" he asked. I could hear how upset he was from his tone of voice. I think it was his worst fear that I was going to see Jason again, and our old feelings would rekindle. Little did he know, he had *nothing* to worry about.

I didn't even know how to begin explaining what I had just gone through. I began stuttering and stammering, and I'm sure I wasn't making any sense.

"Wait, wait, wait. Now *why* are you upset?" he asked, sounding slightly upset himself.

"Tye, I'm not even going to tell you what happened on that stage," I said. "I'm just, emotionally, going through a lot."

"Was it because of what he said?" Tye asked. "Do you still care about him?"

"It's not what it sounds like," I said. "You can't even begin to understand why I'm crying. I'm just so mad. I feel so set up. And I don't need you to do this to me right now."

It bothered him to see me upset over someone else who had broken my heart and made me cry like that. He hadn't wanted me to go and see Jason again. And I'm sure he wondered if I was still in love with Jason, and if I was still emotionally invested in the relationship.

Of course, none of his fears was true. It wasn't Jason. It was the whole process. I had just been totally lured into a trap and lied to. And I knew that people were going to be watching this show, thinking that they knew how it ended, and then there was going to be this huge bombshell. And I didn't know how that bombshell would be received, especially because viewers weren't going to know what had really happened, and they were going to think I got dumped. I had no idea what I was going to look like, or how I was going to come across. I was mad. I was hurt. I was embarrassed. I was confused. And I couldn't explain all of this to Tye. I knew that, even if I tried to explain, nobody would ever be able to know what I was feeling up on that stage except for me. It was such a strange, unique experience to go through.

I laid on the bed, replaying the whole night over and over again. Feelings of anger and humiliation consumed me. *How could I let this happen?* I could only imagine what was going to happen when all my friends and family watched me get engaged, and then watched me get dumped. How was I going to able to face them?

And I couldn't help but be furious with Jason. To not even have the decency to tell me about things before I walked out on that stage, to tell me in front of the world that he was still in love with Molly . . . it was mortifying. And to think this was someone who said he loved me and wanted to spend forever with me.

I guess he meant forever in reality TV years.

eleven

·

BACK TO THE
BEGINNING AGAIN

When I flew home to Dallas the next day, I felt such a mix of emotions. I wasn't sad or heartbroken over Jason, because I had come to see that, in reality, I was never actually in love with him. In the Bachelor Bubble, I had absolutely thought I was in love with him. But that world was far away now. I was actually very relieved that the whole fiasco was finally behind me. Well, I take that back. It still had to *air on national television*. But I was done having to live through it. I figured I could finally move on with my *regular* life and pretend that little hiccup had never happened. The problem was that my real life felt like a total mess again, which is exactly why I had gone on *The Bachelor* in the first place. It seemed like I was caught in a terrible pattern that I couldn't escape. Things would be so great in my life, and then they would always fall apart.

When I got home, it was the strangest feeling, because nobody back home knew what had happened. Not only was I not allowed to tell them what happened, but everyone in America, including many people in my life, were watching the early episodes of *The Bachelor* at that time. This meant that they were right in the middle of seeing me fall in love with Jason. I'm sure my friends could tell what was going on. Their biggest clue was the fact that I didn't want to talk about *The Bachelor* at all. I would either change the topic or avoid it altogether. Even though I knew it would all come out eventually, I decided to prolong the inevitable humiliation for as long as possible.

I went about my normal routine, working at the liquor distribution company and trying to trust Tye enough to build a new relationship with him. I also began to make sense of what had just happened to me. The longer I was outside of the Bachelor Bubble, the easier it was for me to get some perspective. I really think that all of the qualities that had made my girlfriend decide to sign me up for *The Bachelor*—my vulnerability, my low self-esteem, my desperation to be in a serious relationship—were exactly what made me so susceptible to the Bachelor Bubble.

I had even talked about it on my audition tape. Not about Tye specifically, but about how I didn't understand why guys didn't want to be with me, and I didn't know what made them not want to settle down with me. And how all I wanted was to be with somebody who showed me that they wanted to be with me, and yet, simple as that was, I had never found it. I'm sure I had a big bull's-eye on my back during the whole audition process. I'm sure the production people took one look at me and thought they had found their golden girl.

Because I had been so heartbroken over a relationship in which I couldn't freely express my feelings, while I was filming the show, I had said everything I was feeling to Jason *as* I was feeling it. I had no filter. I also came in wanting a relationship so badly that I took any little bit of attention Jason gave me and made it bigger than it was. I let myself get wrapped up in my feelings more than I logically should have. But, of course, I wasn't thinking. I was acting out of pure emotion. And I, honest to goodness, thought I was falling in love with Jason. I really believed that it had become my destiny and that I was meant to leave Tye and go on *The Bachelor* to meet Jason.

Without any prompting, I was just naturally spilling out everything that they wanted from me. It wasn't until the end, when I started to get angry and shut down, that they had to step in and try to make me do things their way. Even though I felt taken advantage of, once I got some distance from the situation, I wasn't as angry as I had initially been. I understood that the show's producers had a job to do. It was just that the way the show was set up, it was inevitable that someone would get hurt. Take a few lonely girls looking for love, mix them up with a little competition under one roof, and put them in the bubble of reality TV, and what do you get: a recipe for disaster! Or, actually, a recipe for complete success, as far as the ratings were concerned.

What I learned throughout the whole process is that you *can* force love, never mind what the song lyrics say! It certainly happened to me!

All it took was a few key elements:

1. *The right frame of mind:* In my case, I was just so broken, and all I wanted was to be loved.

2. *The right chemistry:* Jason and I were certainly attracted to each other enough that we would have had a few good dates in the real world, even if we didn't have the deeper connection for the long haul.

3. *The romance factor:* Don't underestimate the powerful combination of a charming guy and some over-the-top, super-romantic dates.

4. *Friendly producers:* Their encouragement gave all of us girls
   just enough of a shove toward Jason to seal the deal.

Under these circumstances, it was possible to believe in instant
true love and pretty much anything else. The only problem was that
reality did finally conquer fantasy after a while.

Once I made peace with all of this, I could even start to be
grateful for some of the things *The Bachelor* had given me. Not only
had I been able to move to Los Angeles for two months and meet
amazing women, some of whom have become close friends, but I
also grew up in so many ways.

Before the show, I hadn't traveled at all. During *The Bachelor,* I
took more plane trips in two months than I had ever taken in my
entire life. I saw cities I had never seen before. I saw a *country* I had
never seen before! I underwent some once-in-a-lifetime experiences
and collected some great stories to tell my grandkids someday.

I also got a major dose of self-confidence, even if it was sometimes
a little wobbly in the immediate aftermath of *The Bachelor.* When
I was younger, I had developed a very unhealthy approach to
relationships, which I needed to break before I could have a
successful adult relationship.

Ever since my first breakup from Josh at twenty-two, who I had
dated for an epic seven years, I had always tried to hide my pain in
something bigger and better, rather than learning to build myself
up on my own. After that breakup, the bigger and better thing had
been my stint as a Dallas Cowboys Cheerleader. After Tye, I was so
damaged and hurt all over again that I had tried to lose myself in
The Bachelor. I could never get over my breakups because, during
the relationships that preceded them, I had given up so much of
myself and my independence that it actually felt impossible to just

be Melissa on my own. It took me so long to heal from the end of these relationships because, while I was in them, I'd completely forgotten that I had my own wants and needs.

After I got back from *The Bachelor,* I was forced to take a long, hard look at what made a good relationship that was worth a real commitment. I realized that the first requirement of such a relationship was that it shouldn't cause me to lose myself in somebody else. Instead I should find somebody that was my equal, and who I *wanted* but didn't *need.* I once heard a great quote that really speaks to the heart of that sentiment: *Young love: I want you because I need you. Mature love: I need you because I want you.* Before, I had *needed* every relationship I was in. But now I was trying to trust myself enough to believe I could want someone but also feel happy and fulfilled on my own if I didn't have him.

It's amazing how truly independent you can be if you just let yourself be. I hadn't realized how strong I was until I took a step back and analyzed what I had just done. I had moved to a city where I didn't know anyone, roomed with a bunch of strangers, traveled to exotic places, and lived my own adventure—all on my own! And meanwhile, even while I was living it, I had no idea of the scope of my independence. But looking back, I'm pretty proud of myself for being so brave, even if I didn't know it at the time!

These are all lessons that I am grateful for, and I can't imagine that I would be the person I am now without them. But at the time, they weren't easy to understand. I was an emotional wreck, full of questions and doubts. Most difficult of all to face up to was the fact that I had set myself up to go through one of the hardest and most painful experiences of my life on national television. I think I had to forgive myself for this decision as much as I had to forgive Jason and everyone involved in the entire process.

As I made peace with my time on *The Bachelor,* I was also trying to figure out my feelings for Tye. I had come to realize that I was never in love with Jason. I think the fact that I never mentioned to him that I felt like we were having problems, and the fact that he never mentioned it to me, showed the lack of connection between us. At the time, I felt like I was fighting for the relationship, but looking back, I recognized that I never fought absolutely, 100 percent as hard as I could have, because I didn't honestly feel like there was anything real between us that warranted a fight. When I compared how heartbroken I was when Tye dumped me to how nonchalant I was when things ended with Jason, I knew that Jason and I weren't meant to be together. I'm sure that having Tye around at the same time had cushioned the blow some. When the dust settled, I also saw that, somewhere in my heart, I had always wanted Tye all along. You can try pretending to not care about someone you really love, but the charade will always end at some point. I'm a firm believer in fate, and soul mates, and the idea that people who are meant to be together will always find their way back to each other. They may take detours in life, but they always find their way back to their true path.

The good news was that Tye was still trying incredibly hard to get back into my good graces. He kept telling me that he loved me and was going to marry me. I loved hearing what he was saying— it's all I had wanted to hear from him for so long. But my heartbreak over him had been so devastating that I was terrified to allow myself to possibly let him hurt me again. I wanted to believe him, but I couldn't.

But one good thing, in the midst of all this confusion, was that I had come out of the *The Bachelor* with a newfound self-confidence. It gave me the ability to talk to Tye freely, like I always should have been able to do. And this allowed me to express my true feelings, which, at this point, were fear and uncertainty.

"I don't believe you," I said. "I don't trust you."

"Tell me what to do," he said.

"If you really want this to work, you have to show me," I said. "I don't want to hear it anymore, I want to actually see a change. Not a change in you, but a change in us. You know how I feel about you. That's not a secret. My feelings didn't just go away, but I want to see it. I want to see the effort. I want to see the change. I need to see the change."

"I'll do anything," he said.

"I'm not giving you an ultimatum, by any means," I said. "But you need to know that this time, if we get together, we're together. We're making it work. We're in a real relationship, and we're in it for the long haul. I don't emotionally have it in me to go through another breakup with you."

"Absolutely, I'm game," he said.

"And I want to know that, as of now, you think that you're going to be with me forever," I said. "I don't need a ring; I'm not talking about a ring. I'm just talking about a commitment."

"I'm all for it," he said.

No matter what Tye said, given my history with him and the place I was in after what Jason had just done to me, I didn't feel like I could truly rely on Tye. I assumed that after I had refused his advances maybe two or three times, he would give up and move on with his life, and then I could move on with mine.

But Tye was more persistent than ever. And he was a crucial support for me during what was a very painful time. He was incredibly patient, and by being there for me, every day, in all the little ways that he had never been before, he helped me to rebuild my life again. The next thing I knew, I looked at him, and he wasn't the Tye who I had known for the year and a half that we dated. He was this whole different person that would do anything to *be* with me and do anything *for* me. It really was a brand-new relationship. Overnight he became my best friend, and so much more.

We developed a Monday night routine, where we would hang out together at home, *not* watching *The Bachelor,* while all of America was. It was a relief to have his support while I sat cringing at the thought of what everyone I knew was seeing on the show. On the one hand, it was hard to sit in the house, locked up for so long. During the two months that *The Bachelor* was on, we never went on a date, and we literally couldn't go anywhere together. Obviously, it kind of would have blown the ending of the show if someone saw us out together. It was difficult to have to keep our romance secret. But it was also the best thing that could have happened to us, in a way, because during this time, we had no choice but to just sit and talk. We got to know each other on an entirely different level. And I also got clear on what I really wanted. This, right here, right now, was what made me happy, starting a relationship with him. I didn't want to go back on TV and subject myself to public embarrassment again. I wanted to stay in Dallas and build a life with Tye. I suppose it's no secret that this is what I had always wanted.

Tye and I really did start a completely different relationship. Before, our big issue had been communication. He didn't do it, and I didn't know how to do it. I was scared of confrontation. I don't think Tye had ever been in a relationship where his girlfriend argued with him. I had never spoken up to him about things that bothered me. It wasn't worth it to me when I was so afraid of doing anything that might make me lose him. I had kept everything I was feeling inside, and when I finally did let it all out, well, we all know how disastrous *that* ended up being.

But as Tye and I built this new relationship, communication between us was effortless. We never even had to discuss how important it was to be open and honest. We started talking to each other in a different way, and saying things that we had never said before. It just kind of became understood that we both had a responsibility to be up-front about what bothered us. And as soon as we started doing that, none of the things that had troubled us turned out to be a big deal.

Then I realized that just because we disagreed or argued didn't mean that I was being a brat or that I didn't love him. In fact, if he or I was always afraid to tell the other person our opinion, that wasn't a real relationship. The second time around, we could actually ask each other's opinion and be honest if we didn't think something was a good idea. I could make fun of him, and he could make fun of me. We could both say anything and everything to each other. And suddenly we were having this mature, adult relationship. I don't know how it happened exactly, but it did.

It wasn't just the communication that was effortless. Everything was easy. We sat in his living room in our sweats and watched TV or talked. I didn't feel as if I had to make him food or go to Starbucks to get him coffee. I think it was the first time I had ever had a relationship like that, where I just wanted him, and he just wanted me. No muss, no fuss.

I have to admit that I sometimes got a little frustrated because I knew it could have been this easy a year earlier. I realized that I hadn't ever really fallen out of love with Tye. As tough as I had played it with him, it was only because I had to in light of my situation. If I hadn't come back engaged to Jason, I probably would have said my piece to Tye, been mad for a little bit, and then Tye and I would have gotten right back together. But I don't know if our relationship would have been as strong. I really think that nearly losing each other made us so much more appreciative of what we had the second time around, and so much more careful to make sure we never risked it again.

Tye and I were a happy couple again by Valentine's Day. Only this time, it was way different than it had been the year before. Without any prompting from me, Tye planned a Valentine's date for us. Of course, as long as *The Bachelor* was still airing, and America still thought that Jason and I were falling in love and on our way to getting married, Tye and I had to keep our relationship hidden. Luckily, Tye's roommates were all gone that night, so we had the run of the whole condo. He got me dinner—sushi, of course. And then we hooked up his karaoke machine and cranked up the music. I grabbed his roommate's guitar, and Tye got on the microphone. We sang and danced to all of our favorite songs: "Heads Carolina, Tails California," by Jo Dee Messina, "Whatever It Takes," by Lifehouse, and "Apologize" by OneRepublic, among a whole bunch of others. That was our Valentine's Day the year we got back together. And I couldn't have been happier. This was how a relationship should be! Effortless and fun!

While I was over the moon when Tye and I reconciled, my friends Reagan and Stefani were anything but happy. And I could understand why. It was hard for Tye to comprehend the fact that they didn't like him, though. They were very protective of me, and they had seen the emotional mess he had made of me for a year and a half. They figured he'd probably just hurt me again.

I had *always* defended Tye to them, even at my lowest of lows, but they weren't convinced. I knew he didn't mean to hurt me or make me cry. Heck, half the time, he didn't even *know* he was hurting me or making me cry. And he hadn't known because I had kept it from him. I never let him see me angry, hurt, or upset. So how could he be expected to know how unhappy I was? Now that he was aware of how much pain he had caused me in the past, he never wanted to let us get back to that place again.

Although he may not have fully understood why Stefani and Reagan were mad at him, Tye knew it was important to me that they all got along. And he actually took the initiative to make things right with my friends. Big steps here, folks!

Tye made it his mission to prove to my friends that he had never meant to hurt me and that he would never do it again. This meant the world to me. And it showed me how much he really did care about me and our relationship. But Stefani and Reagan were tired of hearing me defend him, and they needed more. For them to believe it, they had to see it come from Tye. Without telling me, he took them out to lunch and told them that he intended to marry me and make me happy. This was the first step in slowly winning them over, which he committed himself to doing over time.

Tye could never give me an explanation of what had changed for him or why. But from that first moment he told me that he intended to marry me, everything was different. He went from zero to everything. He gained a selflessness that he had been lacking before. My needs suddenly came before his needs. Everything he did, he did for us and for our future. The whole time I had known him, he had worked for State Farm Insurance, just like his dad did, and he had planned to open his own agency. He was finally getting ready to open his office, and he included me in the entire process. He asked for my advice. He had me go to meetings with him.

It was a complete turnaround, and it was all instigated by Tye. After I told him what I needed from him to make things work, I didn't say anything else. I didn't make him do anything. He just, overnight, became the person I always knew he was underneath.

One of the most amazing things about Tye is his determination. He sets his mind to something, and by golly, he gets it done! He went to great lengths to prove his love to me. And that included giving up his infamous bachelor life, which he had been living when we dated the first time. Again, this was all his idea. I never once told him what to do. It was important to me that if Tye wanted to make this work, that he made the necessary changes without me forcing anything upon him. I didn't want him to alter who he was or resent me later. I wanted *him* to be the one to initiate the changes. And he did.

One of the biggest leaps Tye made was moving out of his condo—his *bachelor* condo. There had definitely been a point in our early relationship when I thought that nothing would ever be able to tear Tye away from his friends and their playhouse. But this time, it was different. He knew that in order for us to move and grow as a couple, he couldn't keep living his bachelor lifestyle. And it was all his idea. Not only that, he rented an apartment that was within walking distance of mine and a thirty-minute drive to where his friends lived. Talk about making a statement.

Tye and I were really happy, and our relationship was getting stronger day by day. Things were perfect. The time finally came that we had been waiting for: the airing of the final episode of *The Bachelor,* followed immediately by "After the Final Rose." Both were scheduled to air on March 2, 2009. I distinctly remember this date because I had highlighted it on my calendar ever since the taping of "ATFR." After these two episodes were broadcast, Tye and I could finally let everyone know that we were a couple. Finally, no more secrets, and no more sneaking around. *Finally.*

But we first had to get through the night the show aired.

twelve

GOING PUBLIC

had told Tye that I didn't think it was a good idea for him to watch the final episode of *The Bachelor* or the "After the Final Rose" special.

I mean, honestly, who could really stand to watch the person they're in love with get engaged to someone else?

But, of course, he couldn't resist, and he watched both. He got very upset, as I knew he would. I could understand why. It was the same reason that I had been so angry and embarrassed right after we filmed "After the Final Rose." I knew that watching Jason dump me on TV, with me looking as if he'd completely broken my heart and ended the engagement, would disturb him. Even though I had been absolutely open and honest with Tye about the fact that this wasn't actually what had happened, and had explained, instead, all of the emotions I felt about the fact that I had been set up by Jason and the producers, it was difficult for him not to take it personally when he saw me crying on the show and saying, "Why can't I meet anybody? What is wrong with me that I can't fall in love for real?"

That wasn't all that Tye had to hear me say on the show, either. The final episode included footage from the home visit, in which my friends talked about how my ex—yes, as in Tye—never wanted to know them and never really came around. That hurt him, too, and it made him mad because he felt judged by my friends who hadn't met him at that point. It was hard for him to watch me talk about what I had really thought of him and the relationship. It was a truth that I hadn't ever felt comfortable saying to his face, but apparently I had been able to say it to Jason, and a handful of producers, and a camera that brought it into homes across America.

For some reason, Tye and I weren't together the night that the finale and "After the Final Rose" aired, and so I watched both by myself, too. I was worried that they might have edited the footage to make me very unlikeable. As I watched, cringing the whole time, texts started pouring in. Right after the finale aired, my phone *blew up* with text messages:

Oh my god!

Congratulations!

Yay! He's such a great catch!

Then, fifteen minutes later, right after the breakup segment on "After the Final Rose" aired, the text messages continued to come, but they were different this time.

How could he do that?

I'm so sorry!

He didn't deserve you anyway!

I wanted to crawl into a hole and die. As I watched, I knew that everyone in America was thinking that I was this poor girl who had just gotten dumped on national TV, and that I hadn't even seen it coming, and was now heartbroken. Meanwhile, I was thinking that

I didn't want people to believe any of this, *especially* not Tye. I hated the idea that everyone thought I was the victim. As much as I had felt taken advantage of, I didn't feel like a victim, and I didn't want to be seen that way. I had come out of everything with so much confidence, and pity was the last thing I wanted.

Right after both shows aired, I tried calling Tye. I listened to his phone ring and then go to voicemail. Every girl knows what this means: He had hit the Ignore button when he saw my name come up on his phone.

Ouch.

I must have called him twenty times in a row, but he just kept hanging up on me. I knew immediately that he had watched the whole show and that he was angry. As I said, I could understand why he was upset. How many men out there could watch their girlfriend fall in love on TV, get engaged to another man, and still be sane? If I had been in his situation, I don't know if I could have watched him saying things to another girl that he had never said to me before, and essentially falling in love with someone else right in front of my eyes. Even though I told him it wasn't real, that didn't make it any easier for him to see.

Meanwhile, nobody knew that he and I were back together, and so his coworkers and friends had been giving him a hard time. They couldn't believe that, other than a little bit of the first episode that he accidentally saw at the gym, he hadn't watched any of the show. They weren't above rubbing it in his face that he'd apparently lost me to this dude on a dating show. Some of them told him that he wouldn't have wanted to be with me anyway if he had seen what I was doing on the show. After the finale, he was going to face a whole lot more fallout. So I got why he was upset, but I didn't think he had a right to be *that* upset. I mean, I was sitting at home, by myself, humiliated at how I had looked on the show, and my boyfriend was beyond talking to me, he was so upset.

Great. Here we go again. Just when it had felt like all of the puzzle pieces in my life were finally settling into place, something had to come and shake it all up again! I was devastated. Tye and I had survived two months of really hard stuff, while keeping our new relationship a secret the whole time. I gave Tye a lot of credit; it was definitely a hard time for us to get through. But I really thought we had made it. Only maybe we hadn't. Maybe we had gotten this far only to have the show ruin our new start.

To add extra pressure to the situation, I was leaving in two days to be a guest on *The Ellen DeGeneres Show*. When I couldn't get ahold of Tye, I started to panic.

We should at least talk about this!

The next time I called him, and still didn't get through, I left a message:

"I don't want to leave like this because I don't know how we are. I'm going tomorrow, and I want to be able to talk about you on *Ellen*. But if things are not okay between us, you need to tell me, because I just went on TV and professed my feelings for one relationship that wasn't true. I'm not about to go do it again, if I'm going to come home and you're going to say it didn't work out between us."

For twenty minutes, I blew up his phone, calling, hanging up, calling, hanging up. You would have thought I'd have learned my lesson about acting like a crazy stalker, but the thought of losing Tye over this was beyond what I could handle. When I still couldn't reach him, I started to cry. I knew the poo was about to hit the fan, as I like to say. I couldn't imagine what everyone's reaction to my secret TV adventure would be. None of my coworkers had known. None of the cheerleaders had known. As I was trying to deal with all of this, people started calling me and texting me, but all I wanted was to talk to the one person who didn't want to talk to me: Tye.

As I later learned, I wasn't the only one trying to get ahold of Tye that night. The show had aired nationwide, and so everybody was trying to reach him, including his friends, his brother, and his sister. But he wasn't talking to anybody. Finally, his dad called him, and I've always thanked him for what he said to Tye.

"What's going on?" he asked Tye. "Are you okay?"

"No, Dad, I'm not," Tye said.

"Why don't you quit feeling sorry for yourself and for once think about how she feels, and call her and apologize?" Tye's dad said.

Tye's dad was the one person who could always get through to him. The one person who could make him reevaluate a situation. And this time it worked.

The next time I called Tye, he answered. I was so scared about what he was going to say.

"I just need time to get over it," he said. "That stuff was not easy to see or hear. Just give me some time. But I do love you, and I'm not going anywhere."

I've had so many happy moments during my relatively short but incredibly convoluted relationship with Tye. But that was definitely one of the happiest. *Phew! Crisis averted!*

Knowing that our relationship was going to survive this, I became quite sure that there was nothing we couldn't face in the future. I mean, this has got to be one of the hardest things a couple can go through, right? Or at least the most awkward.

Once I knew that Tye and I were okay, I started thinking more and more about everyone else who had watched the show. I was honestly scared to find out what the public reaction was to *The Bachelor,* and to me. I knew the whole backstory, and so I couldn't watch the finale or "ATFR" as an impartial viewer. But people who didn't know everything that had happened probably had a very different reaction. Were people mad at me? Did they hate me? Did I look like a crazy woman on that stage? I had no idea.

While the show was airing, I had sometimes checked out online message boards. I have to admit that I thought it was kind of cool that people were talking about little old me. But now I figured they would be down on me or think I was stupid for making the decisions I had made.

During the time between when ATFR aired on Monday and when I left for Los Angeles to tape *Ellen* on Wednesday, I had purposely avoided all message boards, magazines, and entertainment shows. I had no idea what would happen on *Ellen*. Would she grill me? Would she think I had made a stupid mistake? I was nervous when I thought about what was to come. But at least I was excited to be able to talk about Tye and brag about my relationship with him.

My first visit to *Ellen* was mind blowing. I had never been on a television set before. And I had my own dressing room with my name on the door! I got my hair and makeup done by the artists in the studio. It was pretty cool.

But I was still anxious about what was going to happen. I was shaking when I walked out onto the stage. And then, the crowd *erupted* into applause and chants as I was introduced. I got a huge standing ovation. *What in the world?!*

As I took in the audience's response, I whispered to Ellen that I was nervous.

"Don't be nervous," she said. "Everybody's a friend here."

And she could not have been more right. The audience went nuts when they saw me. The only problem was that they had just seen me get dumped two days before. Meanwhile, on the day that

I appeared on *Ellen,* I had already had those three months since taping ended to put *The Bachelor* behind me and get back on track with my new relationship. So I had pictures of Tye with me, and I was talking about this great new boyfriend I had, and I think it was hard for people to grasp this. Without knowing all of the backstory, they seemed to think that, because I was in a new relationship, I must not have been that heartbroken about Jason, or that Jason and I had just made up our whole relationship for TV. But the overall reaction to my appearance was very positive, and that was such a huge relief after all of those months when I had worried about how bad it would be when the show aired.

The next day, which was a Thursday, I flew back home and went back to work. I did my best to hide out in my cubicle and ignore everyone who wanted to talk about *The Bachelor* that day. But the show wouldn't just go away. My episode had been the most watched *Bachelor* episode EVER, and the production company that made *The Bachelor* approached me that week about being their next Bachelorette. They really wanted me to do it, but the idea could not have been further from my mind. I had no interest in going back to television (note the irony . . . I know).

"No," I said. "I'm not interested."

They kept raising the dollar amount, and raising the dollar amount, and raising the dollar amount. Little did they know, money is not the way into my heart.

"You're not listening to me," I said. "It's not about the money."

They kept trying to convince me.

"I don't trust you anymore," I told one of the producers who called. "I really don't. I came into this in a very vulnerable state, and I feel like I got used for TV. I don't blame you, but what would stop you from using my emotions again to get a good episode?"

As I've said, outside the Bubble, I understood they had just been doing their jobs, and I didn't blame them. But there was no way I was going to put myself back in the Bubble again. If I did, I would have no one to blame but myself for any unhappiness that came from the experience. And I knew there would be abundant unhappiness, especially compared to what I now had with Tye.

They would not give up.

"As the Bachelorette, we would have your back," they said. "You'd be fine." That meant very little to me. I had just seen them throw their Bachelor, Jason, under the bus. The "After the Final Rose" episode had done nothing to make him look like a hero, or even very likeable. So I had no reason to think they would do anything different for me.

I was finally happy. I was with the love of my life. Things were just starting to feel normal again, and I didn't want to tempt fate. The money was not enticing enough to take me away from Tye and make me go through the whole process again. But, honestly, even if I hadn't been with Tye, I don't think I would have done it. The whole experience was so emotionally draining and embarrassing that I couldn't imagine putting myself through anything like it again. I do know that it meant a lot to Tye that I chose not to do *The Bachelorette*. He knew I loved him, but turning down an opportunity like *The Bachelorette* proved to him just how serious I was about us. At the same time, the producers also approached Jillian, another *Bachelor* contestant, about being on *The Bachelorette*. She and I had remained good friends after the show, and so we talked about our decisions.

"I'm not doing it at all," I said. "I know it's a totally different situation for you, but after what I've gone through, not a chance."

Jillian's experience on *The Bachelor* had differed greatly from mine, and so I could understand why she wanted to be the

Bachelorette, and I was happy that she got the opportunity to do it. None of us girls was supposed to be in contact with each other until after *The Bachelor* aired, and we hadn't really, except for the time I got word that Molly and Jason had been talking behind my back. It was such a relief to have the girls back in my life now. Not only had I missed Jillian and Naomi after we left the show, but because of how close we had become, they understood what I had been through better than anyone else, because they had been right there with me. While I could talk to Reagan and Stefani about my experience, they didn't really get how I had fallen for Jason so fast and so hard. But, just like me, Naomi and Jill had been three weeks in and fast in love on the show. It was easier to talk to them about the whole thing because I didn't have to try to explain how I got so wrapped up in it. They understood the process we went through, and the behind-the-scenes reality, and so they were definitely the easiest people for me to talk to throughout that time.

On that Friday morning, after finally convincing the producers that I would not be their next Bachelorette, I was facing down another typical day in my cubicle when my phone rang. It was a woman named Deena Katz, who was a producer for *Dancing with the Stars* (and who would later become my LA mom). She had gotten my number from someone in *Bachelor* production, and she wanted to know if I would be interested in coming to Los Angeles *that night* to be on the show as a last-minute replacement for TV personality Nancy O'Dell, who'd injured her knee during practice.

"Why would you want me?" I asked.

"We think you'd be great," she said.

That was exciting to hear and all, but I wasn't thrilled by the idea of doing TV again after what I had just been through, and they wanted me in Los Angeles that night to rehearse over the weekend so I could dance, LIVE, on television on Monday night. I couldn't believe what I was hearing. This was supposed to be the moment when I got rewarded for all that I had been through by finally getting to spend time with Tye and enjoy our relationship in the open. And here I was, getting asked to leave again.

"I can't do it," I said.

Honestly, I hadn't really seen the show before. I mean, I'd heard of it, and I knew the premise, but I was definitely not an avid watcher. So I didn't really understand the scope of the show at the time, and I wasn't really interested.

I felt like if I went, I would be choosing the show and the entertainment world over my relationship. And I didn't want to do that because I *finally* had the guy I'd been in love with for two years. I didn't want to do anything to jeopardize it. I was sure I was making the right decision. But Deena was equally determined to convince me that I should do the show.

"I'm going to give you thirty minutes to think about it, and I'm going to call you back," she said.

As soon as we hung up, I took my lunch break and called Tye.

"You're never going to believe this," I said. "They called me to be on *Dancing with the Stars*."

"And?" he said.

"Well, I told them no," I said. "I would have to leave tonight, or tomorrow morning, and I'm just not prepared for that."

He was silent for a moment, and then he totally surprised me.

"You should go do this," he said. "Because the worst-case scenario is that you're gone for a week. The best-case scenario is that you're out there for two months, and I get to come out there with you."

Really? Was it that easy? Geez, if Tye was on board, maybe this could be a fun thing for us to get to do.

Deena called me back in thirty minutes. "Have you thought about it?" she asked.

"I have," I said. "I just have a few questions."

"Sure," she said.

"Can my parents come to the show?" I asked.

"Your parents better be at the show, absolutely."

"They can come visit me?"

"Of course," she said, sounding surprised.

"Can I have a cell phone?"

"Yes," she said.

By the end of my questions, she was kind of laughing at me.

"What world did you just come from?" she wanted to know.

I filled her in on everything I had to give up during *The Bachelor.* For all I knew, maybe to be on TV, you had to hand in your cell phones and magazines before you could get in front of a camera. Mild misconception.

And then I told her that, honestly, I was terrified to do reality TV again because of my experience on *The Bachelor.* I described how, during that time, my family and friends were not allowed to talk to me or see me. I couldn't have my cell phone. I was sequestered in a hotel room. I couldn't even use my own name. As exciting as her offer was, I didn't want to go through all of that again on *Dancing.*

"Don't worry, it's nothing like that," she promised.

I believed her, but I was still nervous.

"Can you fly in tonight?" she asked.

"I need one more night," I said. "You just called me half an hour ago!"

I had never watched *Dancing with the Stars,* so just like with *The*

Bachelor, I didn't really know what I was getting into. I just knew that being swept out of my cubicle to go do the show was like being a princess in a fairy tale. I spent that last night with Tye and his family. Tye and I sat there on his computer at his house, looking up the *Dancing* cast, learning which celebrities were on the show for the first time and picking out dancers we hoped would be my partner.

The next morning, I was on a plane to Los Angeles, and that afternoon, I met my dance partner, Tony Dovolani, for the first time. In two days, on Monday night, we would be dancing live together in front of millions of viewers. Strangely, I wasn't nervous about whether or not I would be able to learn the dance in time. I'm naturally able to hear music and count out the beat so that helped me to master it more quickly. Also, I got lucky, and our first dance was the waltz. Because I had a ballet background growing up, the waltz was probably the easiest dance for me to learn on the fly.

Knowing that we only had two days to master the routine, Tony also watered down the dance quite a bit. What did take me a while to get used to was dancing with a partner. Especially because some of the later dances, like the rumba, got a little, shall we say, *intimate,* and I'm very goofy when it comes to any kind of sexy stuff.

That first day, Tony and I practiced for about four hours, and then they brought in wardrobe to fit me for my costume. I was in awe when I saw the dress I was going to be wearing. It was a wild moment when I realized that I was actually going to be on *Dancing with the Stars.*

Me!

I couldn't even begin to grasp the scope of what I was doing.

On Sunday we again practiced for another four hours. By that point, Tony and I both felt like we were doing pretty well. I didn't want to overpractice, and I didn't want to psyche myself out, so we decided to stop while we were ahead.

"All I want to do is have fun," I told Tony. "You're coming back here next season. I'm probably going back to my life in Dallas. This is the one little window of this life that I'm going to get, and so I don't care if we go out and completely bomb. I don't care if we forget a routine. I don't care if my shoe falls off. I just want to remember this whole experience and have the best time possible."

And that's just what I did.

On Monday night, I went to the studio to get ready to tape the show, and when I got to hair and makeup, they sat me next to Holly Madison. I was freaking out because I was used to watching her on TV, and here we were, getting our hair and makeup done together. I'm sure I would have been even more starstruck if they'd had us with the rest of the cast, which included Denise Richards and Lil' Kim. But the producers were keeping it hush-hush that Holly and I were the replacements for the two contestants who had dropped out at the last minute, so they kept us separate from the rest of the cast until it was time for us to dance. This did add a little bit of stress to the night because it also meant that Tony and I couldn't go out and practice on the stage, like all of the other couples were able to do. He and I got one secret run-through on the stage, just so I could see it for the first time. But that was it.

And then we went live.

I'm not sure why I didn't feel more nervous or unprepared than I did, but I don't think it ever really sunk in how *BIG* this was. I had never done live TV before, and I didn't think about the fact that it was the number one show in America at the time. I was very naïve about how significant the moment was.

If someone called me today and asked me to do the same thing with so little time to prepare, I don't know that I would do it. But I think that in that moment, my innocence actually worked to my advantage, because it kept me from overthinking the situation and getting stressed out. The only thing that I was worried about was how the public was going to react to me following "After the Final Rose." I had no idea what people had been saying about me, or how they would feel about suddenly seeing me on *Dancing with the Stars*. I had purposely avoided hearing or reading about the public's reaction to the finale, which had aired just a week earlier. For all I knew, everyone in America hated me.

After everything I had just been through, I really didn't feel emotionally ready to handle people being nasty. As Tony and I stood in the wings, waiting for our cue, I confessed my fears to him.

"I'm terrified we're going to go out there, and people are going to boo us," I said. "Or that we're going to be the first couple voted off because nobody likes me."

Tony tried to reassure me, and then I heard our names announced as the next couple to dance, and it was time go out. Literally, the second they said my name as Tony and I walked out on stage, the audience went crazy. Viewers at home saw the show cut to a pretaped package that included footage of Tony and me practicing over the weekend. But in the studio, every single person was standing up, clapping and cheering for me. I heard women yelling my name. I could actually see people crying from the stage. I got these huge tears in my eyes. I couldn't believe that all of that warmth and support were for me. It still makes me tear up when I think about it.

Next thing I knew, I heard our music starting, and off we went. I didn't think twice about anything. My body took over and I went into my Dancing Bubble, which is a good kind of bubble! I didn't notice the cameras or feel anxious at all. I was just looking at Tony and having a great time.

As soon as we hit our ending position, and the last beat of music played, I started crying again. *Oh my gosh! We did it! We did it!* It was all so overwhelming.

The crowd *erupted*! And it was all for us. I couldn't help my tears; I felt so proud of what we had just accomplished after only eight hours of practice.

I had gone from this awful pit in my life three months ago to not only being so happy personally, but to also being on the number one TV show and having everyone cheering for me right after Tony and I had done a really good job. After the dark place I had come from, it was such an indescribable feeling to see a reaction like that coming from people I'd been expecting to boo me.

After Tony and I were done with the show, I went back to my trailer, and I had all of these messages—the text messages alone numbered fifty-six—from my friends and other people back home:

"Oh my god, you're on the show!"

"I just saw you on *Dancing*!"

I hadn't been able to tell anyone except for Tye and my parents that I was doing the show—luckily, all of these reality TV experiences have made me very good at keeping secrets—and so the rest of the people in my life had no idea where I was and what I was doing. At least, not until they turned on their television sets that night and saw me waltzing across the stage with Tony. I'm sure it was just as crazy for them to see me there as it was for me to actually *be* there! The whole thing had happened so quickly that neither Tye nor my parents had been able to get time off from work to be there, but Tye told me later that he was at the gym that night, and when he saw me on the TV, he couldn't help shouting encouragement to me.

I think for everyone else, who had watched me on *The Bachelor,* it was a relief for them to see that I was okay, and that even though I had been knocked down, I had gotten right back up and gone on with my life in an even bigger and better way than before. I think there were a lot of women out there who watched what I went through on "After the Final Rose" and felt like they had been through the exact same thing but never had the chance to tell off the guy who did it to them. And so they were inspired to see that it had all worked out for me in the end. And had it ever worked out for me!

The first episode of *Dancing with the Stars* aired on March 9, and my birthday was two days later. The year before had been probably my worst birthday *ever,* spent with my best friends, yes, but heartbroken and directionless at Medieval Times in Dallas. What a difference a year makes. For this birthday, I had dinner at a swanky restaurant with Deena Katz and my dance partner Tony, as well as Apple cofounder Steve Wozniak and ABC executive John Saade. I couldn't believe how much had changed—and all for the better.

My life quickly developed a new routine. From Wednesday to Sunday, my days were jam-packed with practice, then an interview, then a fitting in wardrobe, then another quick interview, then another practice, then a trip to the stage to mark the dance for our live performance, and then maybe I'd go pick up some new shoes. Monday was show day, and Tuesday was elimination day, during which I always loved going into the studio and getting my hair and makeup done and putting on the costumes, which were amazing.

Even compared to what I was used to from cheerleading, the practice was grueling. For the first two weeks, I couldn't move by the end of the day because I was using muscles that I'd never used before, and I was *so sore*! But it was a great life, and I had it easy. I didn't have another job when I did *Dancing with the Stars,* like so many people who were trying to record an album or film a sitcom while they were doing the show. I couldn't understand how these people did it. Even just doing *Dancing,* I got up at seven o'clock in the morning, didn't go to bed until ten at night, and felt like every moment in between was jam-packed.

But I loved every second of the show, and it was such a fun period for me in general. Tye had some downtime before opening his own insurance agency, and so he moved out to LA with me. The show put us up in a cute little apartment and gave us use of a car. When I was done with my obligations for the day, Tye would pick me up, and we'd try a new restaurant or coffee shop, go see a movie, or just play around. It was such a carefree time in my life that I felt like I was being rewarded for the fact that I hadn't given up, even when I had gone through such a bad period right before that.

My parents came out for every episode, which was especially fun for my mom, because she was a really big fan of the show. Tye's parents also came to LA several times, as did a couple of our friends. They all enjoyed the experience of getting dressed up and coming out to be a part of a live TV show as it was taped, seeing the celebrities, and marveling over how the whole process worked and the fact that the set was so much smaller than it looked on TV. They all cheered me on when I danced, and then came back to my trailer after the show, so we could go out to dinner afterward. Plus, they had the excitement of being out in Hollywood, and I still don't know what any of us were doing out in Hollywood, *including me*!

Tony and I developed a very special relationship. About two weeks in, he already had a good grasp of how I was as a dancer. In practice, I didn't perform. I learned the steps by walking through them, so my body could develop the muscle memory to internalize the routine by Monday night. Come Monday night, though, I performed my heart out. I came to know Tony, too, and learn that he was also more subdued during practice, but on Monday nights, he threw me a lot higher in the air. When we performed, it was almost like a completely different dance. The time we spent practicing from Wednesday to Sunday allowed us to learn the steps and how to mesh with each other. And then, on Monday, we both went out and we both just—*BAM*—turned it on.

I adapted really well to both practicing and performing, so Tony soon knew that he didn't have to remind me to smile, or tilt my head up on a certain part, or *NOT* focus on the audience. And he did a really good job of choreographing things that he and I could pull off, and picking out great music and costumes that I really liked. We had a special relationship, almost like a brother and sister, where we could joke with each other and make fun of each other, and if I was having a bad day, he knew how to get me out of it, and vice versa.

Five days is not a lot of time to learn a new style of dance and memorize the entire routine, plus do costume fittings and interviews. It was grueling. And that's why, usually around weeks eight and nine, people started to kind of crack. They cried a lot. They talked about how exhausted they were. I never got that worn down. But as I said, it was a pretty carefree time in my life, and I managed to stay focused on having fun, even as week after week went by without us getting eliminated, and we got closer and closer to winning the show.

Tony and I developed a routine on Monday night. We always knew when we were going on. We never watched the people who danced before us, but while they were dancing, we got ourselves into position and psyched ourselves up. When the music started, I always went out on such a huge adrenaline high that it was almost like I became a different person for the two or three minutes I was onstage. Even though I'd only had five days to practice, I always knew the routine, so I just let my body take over. That's when that muscle memory kicked in. As anyone who's watched the show knows, contestants never go out there, forget their steps, and freeze completely. All of the contestants have always practiced enough that they know what they're doing. It's just that some people can turn it on at the last second and some people can't. Luckily, that wasn't hard for me. I always felt like my only job was to really let the personality out. And I could do that. Beyond that, I just made sure to have fun! And I always did.

here definitely is something called "fifteen minutes of fame," and during this time, I was smack-dab in the middle of mine. I was immediately thrown into a whole new world: the world of celebrities and paparazzi. Because *Dancing with the Stars* was so popular, and people were still talking about what had happened on the "After the Final Rose" special, I got a lot of attention during the time I was in LA for *Dancing*. It baffled me that people cared so much about what I was doing. Paparazzi waited outside our dance studio hoping to get a shot. And let me tell you, it is *weird* having people follow you around taking your picture! There is nothing natural about it!

To this day, I'm still not used to paparazzi (thankfully, we don't have any in Dallas!), but I was especially uncomfortable around them when I was first thrust into the spotlight. I was particularly freaked out one evening when I was heading home from practicing with Tony, and I noticed a car following me. I recognized it as one of the paparazzi cars that parked in the parking lot of the dance studio, hoping to get pictures of all the celebrities leaving practice.

Oh, great.

I started taking detours, going in and out of random little neighborhoods, trying to lose him. But he was relentless and stayed right behind me. I started getting upset, because I was going *home*! I didn't want them to know where I lived! I kept weaving in and out of traffic, going in and out of parking lots, doing everything I could to lose him—or at least give him the hint that I knew he was following me. It didn't work. Panicking, I called Tye for help.

"Baby! I'm getting followed by paparazzi!" I said. "And I just want to go home! What do I do?"

I'm not sure what I thought Tye could do to help. He was two thousand miles away in Dallas, and neither of us had ever had to deal with an issue like this before.

"What can I do?" he replied. "I can't really do anything. But are you okay?"

I felt bad for worrying Tye when he was so far away, but he suggested that I try calling Tony.

Brilliant! So I called Tony and told him what was going on. Thankfully, he was right down the street and said he'd meet me at the coffee shop next to my apartment. When I pulled in, the paparazzi car parked behind me. Tony arrived about five minutes later. When Tony saw us, he got out of his car, went up to the car, leaned in and talked to the paparazzo.

"You're freaking her out a little bit," he said. "She's not used to this. She's not going anywhere. She's just trying to go home. And she doesn't want you to follow her home."

"Oh, yeah, absolutely," the guy said. "I didn't mean to scare her." And just like that, he drove off. I was so relieved.

Wow, that was easy.

It was great to know that Tony was there for me, especially

because he was really all I had in LA while Tye was still in Dallas. Although it was a small gesture on Tony's part, it had meant the world to me.

During the second week of *Dancing with the Stars,* I was on the cover of *People* magazine, which was a totally surreal experience. Around this time, I first realized that the public really knew who I was. When Tye and I went out to have coffee or go to the grocery store, people started coming up to talk to me about the show, and it became increasingly common for paparazzi to follow us.

The first time it happened when Tye and I were together, it felt totally crazy and weird. This was during the second week, after Tony and I had done our waltz, and Tye had moved to LA to be with me. He and I were in the car on our way to the dance studio so he could drop me off for rehearsal, when Tony called me.

"Hey, I just want you to know, there's paparazzi out front," he said.

I was surprised. But after the paparazzi debacle that had just happened, I thought it was such a sweet gesture for Tony to call and warn me.

"Really?" I said. "What should I do?"

"Don't talk to them, don't do anything, just come in," he said.

"Okay," I said.

I was nervous. I had never dealt with paparazzi, or even really seen them, except on TV and that one time Tony had to shoo them away for me. When Tye and I walked into the studio, I remember trying so hard not to make any eye contact. I'd covered the label of the Red Bull I was holding, because on *Bachelor,* we had to tape over all labels. And so, for some reason, I thought that was true in the outside world, too. From the time we got out of the car to when we went inside the studio, they filmed us with a video camera and took a bunch of still pictures, too. It's was such an awkward feeling, and I had no idea how to behave.

Do I smile? Do I wave? Do I act for the cameras? Or do I pretend they're not there? Oy!

After that, it became a regular occurrence. The paparazzi knew where we practiced and at what times, and they were always there before and after practice. They also followed us home. It just kind of became . . . not normal exactly, but that was just how life was. I went to practice, or out to brunch with Tye or a girlfriend, knowing there would be paparazzi waiting for me.

I soon figured out how they always knew where I was (and not just me, but the entire cast of *DWTS*). Remember how I said the show put us in an apartment while I was in LA? Well, we were *all* in the same apartment complex—and I'm sure it's the one they use every season. It wouldn't take a rocket scientist paparazzo to figure this out. So all they had to do was wait outside the complex for one of the cast members to exit the parking lot, and—BAM they were found out! And since the rental car I was in was *bright red,* I was easily discovered! While I got used to this attention, I was always a little uncomfortable with it.

I also got irritated sometimes, when I wasn't in the mood to have my picture taken. It was frustrating to know that they were trying to get a bad shot that would embarrass me, while they were going to get paid for it. But I was lucky in that no one ever crossed the line or was ever mean to me. No one ever tried to get a really nasty shot or make me say something terrible. When I became more used to it, I learned to feel flattered and smile. That way they could get their picture, and then I could go on with my life, while remembering the whole time that this was just LA, and my real life in Dallas was nothing like this and never would be.

My parents actually had it worse than I did during the time that *Dancing with the Stars* aired. This was at the height of the show's popularity, and so it was earning a lot of attention. On top of that, it always seems like there are one or two contestants who really get a lot of notice each season. For some reason, during my season, I was one of the contestants who people got curious about. It was crazy. Somehow, someone from my high school was contacted, and my yearbook photos were published in a tabloid. And my poor parents got swarmed. One tabloid magazine, in particular, kept going around their neighborhood, and coming up to their house, trying to get pictures of me. People even started going through their trash looking for stuff. Now, remember, my parents didn't want to be on *Bachelor,* so they weren't exactly the kind of people who were going to be inviting a tabloid magazine in to take pictures. So they actually moved. They did the whole thing very quietly, and luckily, their house sold before they even had to put up a For Sale sign, so no one knew that they had relocated.

The whole experience was incredibly unreal for my entire family. And I think everyone at home thought it was crazy, especially a lot of my coworkers, who had seen me at work on Friday, just like normal. And then when Monday night came around, and there I was on *Dancing with the Stars,* I'm sure they were sitting in front of their televisions, unable to believe their eyes.

I could hardly believe some of the things that were happening to me, either. Just take the fact that I had gone from being a complete unknown to opening a magazine and seeing my face in it. One of the first really cool moments I experienced was when I made the *Us Weekly* Hot Hollywood list! That meant that we got to go to the party celebrating the launch. It was a red carpet event—my *first* red carpet event!

How exciting!!

Tony got a Phantom for the night, so there Tye and I were, riding to a Hollywood party in the back of a Phantom with Tony and his wife. Next thing we knew, we were walking down a red carpet. Now, I had never done a red carpet before in my life, so I got totally overwhelmed when I faced that sea of lights.

What do I do? How do I stand? How do I pose? Am I smiling too big?

And it showed in the pictures that were taken that night. I laugh whenever I look back at them, because I appear so incredibly unsure. But who could blame me? This was nothing I was even thinking about three months earlier. It was amazing how quickly, and how dramatically, my life had changed.

Once we got inside the party, the room was nothing but celebrities, and Tye and I were completely starstruck. Many of the dancers from *Dancing with the Stars* were there, so we had our own little section, but Tye and I could never be found there. We were walking around the whole time, whispering to each other.

"Oh my gosh, that's Jay Manuel from *America's Next Top Model*!"

"Oh my gosh, there are the Kardashians!"

The Kardashians were just sitting at their table, and we were totally staring at them. We couldn't help ourselves. We never felt like we fit in. Even now that I've been in the public eye longer, I never assume that someone knows who I am, and I *really* didn't back then. So at that party, when I saw somebody, I'd stick out my hand and introduce myself, even though I knew exactly who they were.

Holly Madison was there. We had danced together for several weeks, but she left the show fairly early, and there had been two or three weeks between then and this party, so I had no idea if she remembered me or not. When I saw her, I stopped to chat.

"Holly, hi, Melissa, I danced with you on *Dancing,*" I said.

"Oh my gosh, yes," she said and gave me a hug.

I couldn't believe it, but I learned very quickly that there are no introductions in the celebrity world because everybody knows who everybody else is. Or at least it's understood that everyone probably knows one another. Very weird. That was hard enough to fathom, but it was even stranger for me when people started approaching *me*. The first person who ever recognized me and came up to talk to me was T.O.! You know, football star Terrell Owens, who had played for the Dallas Cowboys! Clearly, this was a *big* deal for me and Tye. We both just stood there, trying to act normal, like this should be happening, and he should know exactly who we were. But as soon as he walked away, we lost it.

"Terrell Owens just came up and talked to us!" I said.

We were on cloud nine! It was a very cool moment.

The one thing that bothered me about being in the public eye at the time had to do with my relationship with Tye. As far as the TV viewing public was concerned, Jason and I had just broken up on Monday, and now, here it was the following Monday, and I was already in a brand-new relationship. And not only that, but I was so happy and so in love. Many people couldn't understand how I could have moved on so quickly, and they felt like I had played the victim and acted heartbroken when I had never really loved Jason. Of course, the problem was that they didn't understand the real time line. And I never had the chance to publicly explain that we had filmed "After the Final Rose" nearly three months after taping for *The Bachelor* ended, or that Tye and I had this whole long history *way* before I ever even met Jason or got caught up in the Bachelor Bubble.

My relationship was great, my work life was amazing, and I had my family's full support. I couldn't have been happier. The only problem was that, with how grueling the show was, I was getting tinier and tinier as the season went on. I mean, think of how much you have to eat when you are literally working out eight hours a day, straight! It's nearly impossible to keep weight on! No matter how much I ate—and just ask Tye, I can eat—I couldn't seem to make the weight stick, and I became increasingly fragile. My body was definitely getting put through the ringer, and I could feel it starting to shut down on me.

The second to last week, we did the Argentine tango, which was a dance where we were allowed to do lifts. So Tony was constantly lifting me, and twisting me, and turning me. Well, on the last lift of the dance, during one of our final practices, I felt a huge *POP* across the right side of my back. When Tony put me down, I couldn't take a deep breath, and I was in a lot of pain. But I tried to work through the pain, thinking it couldn't be *that* bad of an injury. When I decide to do something, I become very stubborn and determined, and so I kept on practicing, even though it hurt *a lot.*

I sucked it up and went through with the live show on Monday night. But as soon as the dance was over, I collapsed in pain. Tony had to help me over to the judges table because I could barely walk, let alone breathe.

Not good.

The next day, we started our new dance for the next week. It was the jive. We did okay in practice, but the jive is not like the waltz, which is very slow and elegant. It's constant and very high energy. It literally felt like we were running a race for three minutes. I was having trouble breathing, and I was worried that I wouldn't be able to make it through the routine when we filmed the show on Monday night.

Tony finally suggested that we go to a doctor, just to make sure that everything was okay. I reluctantly agreed. I didn't want to admit that something could be wrong. We had come so far in the competition, and I didn't want to have to give up because of a stupid injury.

The doctor ended up taking X-rays, and he came back with bad news. He pointed to the film he had just hung on the wall. "It looks like you have three hairline fractures on your right rib cage," he said.

Oh my gosh! Fractures? Ribs? What?

"So . . . what does this mean?" I asked. "I mean, we have to practice. Can I still dance?"

Even as I asked the question, I feared his answer.

He sighed and shrugged.

"I mean, you can," he said. "It is very unlikely that dancing further will actually *break* your ribs. So it's really just about pain management. Because injuries to the ribs are always painful, this is going to be the largest hurdle."

All I heard from what he said was: You can.

Done! We will keep practicing then!

And so we practiced as usual, but by the time the live show came around, I was in terrible pain. I was told that after we finished our rehearsal on the stage, I could go get a shot that would numb the pain temporarily. I thought that sounded like a great idea and decided to go ahead and do it.

Tony and I went through rehearsal, and right after that, I left for the hospital to get my shot. Tye and Tony both came with me. The doctor had me lay on my side, and he injected the first shot. Yes, I said first shot. Because I had three fractures, I had to get three shots. Now this was nothing like how a needle stings when it goes into your skin. This was excruciating, like bee stings going all the way up and down my body. I was cringing and crying. Tye was holding my hands and Tony was looking on, helpless. And I still had two shots to go.

"You need to wait just a second while I kind of recoup," I said.

I sat up, and my chest hurt when I took a deep breath, which seemed odd. But I didn't think too much about it—yet.

"Are you ready to get the next one?" the doctor asked.

"Yeah," I said. "But if you can just do the next two at the same time, it'll be a lot easier for me."

So he gave me the next two shots at the same time, and, again, it was the worst kind of pain. I rolled back over and sat up.

"My chest really, really hurts," I said. "Like it hurts to take a deep breath."

"Just sit here for a minute," he said. "It should get better."

Then the doctor left the room, and Tye, Tony, and I sat there together. After maybe thirty seconds, I looked at them both because I was really scared.

"Something's wrong," I said. "Something's going on. I feel like I can't catch my breath. My neck is either swelling or closing. I can't take a deep breath."

I sat on the table struggling to breathe. Talk about panic!

And then, I stopped talking because I couldn't talk anymore. Tye and Tony were both freaking out and called the doctor back in as quickly as they could. Only when the doctor arrived, he didn't come over to help me. He took one look at me and started yelling.

"Call 911!," he told Tony.

What?? Did the DOCTOR just say to call 911?? Aren't we at the hospital?

"Get out the defibrillators," he said to Tye.

I've never seen a look of terror like I saw on Tye's face at that moment. He started fumbling around trying to get the defibrillator out of the plastic casing it was in on the wall, which was sealed tight.

Now I was really scared. But I couldn't say anything at this point, so I just looked at Tye and tried to communicate with my eyes: *Help me! Please, do something, because I can't breathe!*

As anyone who has ever had an episode where they couldn't breathe or catch their breath knows, it is literally the scariest feeling in the world. Just pure terror. After about a minute, I could feel everything kind of opening back up again. And I could finally relax enough to look around me again. Tye and Tony were both crying in opposite corners of the room. I tried to take small breaths, but my back still really hurt. I looked at the doctor.

"Am I having some kind of an allergic reaction?" I asked.

"No, that's not it," he said.

But he never actually told me what it was that had happened to me. To be honest, I didn't care at this point. Even though I still had the stabbing pain in my chest and back, I could breathe, and that's all that mattered to me.

The doctor gave me some candy to suck on to make sure everything was still moving okay through my esophagus. Thirty minutes later, he let me go. I thought this was a little strange, because my ribs still hurt as much as they had before, only now I couldn't take a deep breath. It felt like I was being stabbed in the chest and in the back. But I figured he was a doctor, so he knew what he was doing.

Tony and I arrived back at the studio, and it was now about an hour until we went live. I was so nervous because I actually felt worse than I had before we'd left for the hospital.

"Tony," I said. "I can't really take a deep breath right now. I can't even talk."

We told the producers what was going on, and they had us go out on the stage one more time to see if I could get through the routine. I danced for maybe twenty seconds, and then I just collapsed. They had to carry me offstage. My parents and Tye saw the whole thing and were terrified.

The producers brought in another doctor, just to get a second opinion. And lo and behold, he told us that the first doctor had punctured my lung! Let me repeat: punctured my lung! What I had felt was the numbing medicine as it went up my esophagus and made it so I couldn't feel anything. And the sharp stabbing pains I was feeling was from the air that had escaped my lungs and entered my chest cavity. (Apparently, your body is not supposed to have air floating around in it.)

The whole thing was really scary, especially because I learned afterward that it can be really dangerous when a person's lung is punctured, and I had no idea. Luckily, the second doctor was really good. He came over to my apartment several times that night to check on me and make sure I could still walk and everything.

Obviously, I wasn't allowed to perform that night, and the show went on without me. But no one wanted to make a big deal out of it, so I was told to say that I couldn't dance because I had just bruised my ribs. The whole experience was really frustrating because I absolutely would have danced if I'd only had bruised ribs, even though I'm sure it would have hurt some. And I couldn't say anything about what was really going on. All I could do was sit in the wings and watch the show go on without me. Because I was not there to dance live, producers showed the audience a video of our last rehearsal on the stage (right before we'd left for the hospital). And that's what the judges had to score. Needless to say, Tony and I were at the very bottom of the leaderboard after that night.

I was so nervous going into the elimination night the next day. I just had a feeling that Tony and I were going home. And not only that, I couldn't even explain *why* I wasn't able to dance. I'm sure the audience thought that I was just being dramatic and wanted sympathy or something. I was really stressed and upset.

"I just don't want to go home this way," I said to Tony. "I want to go home because I didn't dance well enough, or I had a bad day. I don't want to go home because I wasn't even given the chance to go out and prove myself."

Tony and I stood on that stage—in the bottom two—and clung to each other tightly. It was definitely the most nerve-wracking moment of the whole show. But, thankfully, we somehow made it through. And, more than ever, I was determined to dance better than ever.

Tony and I actually returned that next week and scored our first 30 on our samba! Talk about coming back with a vengeance! We were just one week away from the finals at this point, and I was so excited to have made it that far! I was mentally, physically, and emotionally exhausted—as everyone on the show was at this point—but we could definitely see that the end was near.

The night of the *DWTS* finale, the vibe was much different backstage—at least between Tony and me. Of course we wanted to win, but at this point, we were so excited to have made it this far that we just wanted to have fun. Regardless of how we placed, this would be our last time out on the stage together. So we decided to just have a great time and make the most out of it.

I had some pretty steep competition, too. Gilles Marini from *Sex and the City,* and Olympic gold medalist Shawn Johnson. I couldn't complain about losing to either of them, because they both really were phenomenal. By the end of the night, I was just so relieved.

We were done!

After twelve weeks—ten to twelve hours a day, seven days a week—we were done! The three finalists were all standing on stage waiting to hear our fate, and for the first time on an elmination night, I wasn't nervous at all. Tony and I couldn't make it any further. There wasn't another show after this one—we had literally gone to the end of the line. So first place, or third place, I was ecstatic.

As it turned out, Tony and I did get third place. Gilles got second place, and our little Shawn got first. There was a huge celebration on stage, with confetti and everything! And we were done!! I wasn't going to have to wake up at seven o'clock for an eight-hour practice tomorrow! My feet and body could finally heal!

Ahhhh!

The onstage celebration ended quickly for us, because all the finalists and their guests got to fly to New York City on the private Disney jet. Yes, folks, I said private plane! I mean, who does that unless they're Mariah Carey or Tom Cruise?! Well, we did! To be honest, though, the only reason we took a private plane was to be in New York in time to appear on *Good Morning America* and *Live! with Regis and Kelly* the next morning. That was a whirlwind: *Dancing* was done filming around eight o'clock. We flew out of Los Angeles by ten o'clock that night, and we were in New York and ready to go on the air by six o'clock the next morning.

Phew!

The three finalists and our dance partners were sitting on *GMA* talking to the hosts when Robin Roberts and Diane Sawyer surprised each of us with special video messages. The one for Shawn Johnson was from her gymnastics team. The one for Gilles Marini was from his kids. I figured mine was going to be from Tye or my family. But when they started to play my video, all of the sudden, Derek Jeter popped up on the TV screen. When I heard him say my name, I lost it! I don't even remember what he said to me because I was making such a big fool of myself. I loved Derek Jeter, as in I used to say that he was my future husband. Before I met Tye, of course. I couldn't believe that he had agreed to tape a special message just for me. Plus, the producers gave me a ball and a hat that he had signed. My life really was too good to be true!

fourteen

DREAM JOB

Things got even better after *Dancing* because Tye and I finally got to spend some time together. The week after the *Dancing* finale was done, we took our first big vacation together, just the two of us, to St. Lucia. The funniest thing happened while we were there. We were staying at a resort, and I guess the staff had heard that some TV personality was going to be a guest at the hotel.

I had started getting recognized occasionally while *Bachelor* was airing, which I really didn't like because of how that whole situation turned out. I was much happier being known as the girl from *Dancing with the Stars* than the girl from *The Bachelor*. More and more people had started coming up to me while I was eating, or shopping, or taking a walk. They were always very nice, and what they usually said was that they felt like they knew me. I had a lot of people either just start asking me questions about relationships, or tell me their thoughts on what had happened to me. I always wanted to tell them that, if they only knew my backstory, they'd really have something to say, but I decided it was better to keep my personal life as private as possible.

Anyhow, I had become more used to being recognized by the time Tye and I went to St. Lucia. When we got to the resort where we were staying, all of the butlers and waiters and staff said the same thing when Tye and I walked by:

"TV celebrity! TV celebrity!"

And they'd be pointing and smiling at us; it was really cute!

I'd just smile and wave. It really was flattering that the staff in St. Lucia knew who I was. Sometimes they had another chant when we passed by:

"Movie star! Movie star!"

I thought it was adorable! They thought I was a movie star!

Ha! I'll take it!

Even though I clearly was not a movie star, Tye and I never corrected them. We just laughed and smiled. I mean, come on! It *is* funny!

At one point, one of the employees ran up to Tye and started pumping his fists in the air and chanting, "Move that bus! Move that bus!"

Huh?

Tye and I immediately cracked up laughing! Apparently, they thought that Tye was Ty Pennington, the host of *Extreme Makeover: Home Edition*! And they had no idea who I was. We thought this was hilarious! But there were a few people who worked at the resort who did recognize me. And it baffled us how these natives of St. Lucia knew who I was. That really helped me to grasp how big the scope of *Bachelor* and *Dancing* was. These shows weren't just something people were watching in Los Angeles and Dallas. People were seeing them all over the world.

When we went home to Dallas, I decided not to go back to my old job at the liquor distribution company. I figured that after everything I had just gone through, now was the time in life to find something that I really enjoyed doing. I wasn't necessarily in any hurry to go back to finding a new job and work, and so I was looking forward to having some down time. At least for a little bit. Tye was in the final stages of opening his office, and that meant going back and forth between Dallas and Austin quite a bit. Because he had been so great about picking up and going to LA to be with me during *Dancing,* I decided to do the same for him, and we traveled back and forth together for a few months.

I was perfectly happy with my little vacation, but it didn't last. About two weeks after I had been on *Good Morning America,* I got a phone call from Deena Katz, who had become my mentor, manager, and second mother during the time I worked with her on *Dancing.*

"Are you sitting down?" she said. "I've got some amazing news! *GMA* wants you to be a correspondent for them!"

"Are you kidding me?" I said.

GMA wants me?! Do they know I don't have ANY experience in this field?!?

"No, what they want you for is fun, lighthearted morning pieces," she said. "You go in, have fun, show your personality, go live, and go home."

I couldn't believe it. I was a finance major! I didn't have any experience informing the public of anything. I had no idea how *real* television worked—I had never even actually conducted an interview!

Maybe this is because of the way I reacted when I went on the show with the other DWTS finalists, and I made such a scene about Derek Jeter merely saying my name . . . ?

So maybe they did just want me to be myself. I could be myself. That was for sure.

"Okay, let's do it!" I said.

Just like everything else in my life around that time, it all happened very quickly. My first assignment was that weekend. It was a piece on comedian Steve Harvey.

Steve Harvey?! My first go at this, and they are throwing me right in!

As we taped the segment, I couldn't quite comprehend what I was actually doing. It took all day to shoot, and it was so much fun! Then, that night, I flew to New York to "track" the story. Tracking is when you provide the voice-overs for the segment. After tracking the piece, I went to my hotel room (conveniently located across the street from the *GMA* studios), and tried to get a good night's sleep for my first live segment the next morning.

My alarm went off at five o'clock, and off to the studio I went. I got my hair and makeup done (always makes you feel fantastic!), and got some notes on how the segment would go. I was told I'd be talking with Robin Roberts and Diane Sawyer.

Um, excuse me? Who?! Are these people actually my coworkers now? Un-believable!!

Walking out onto the *GMA* set was an unbelievable experience. At the time, they had a live audience in the studio, and they were all smiling and clapping for me.

This is a good start: At least they're not booing.

My first live segment flew by! I chatted with Robin and Diane for a minute, then the piece aired, and we talked for a minute afterward about the story. And just like that, it was over. But that's all it took to get me hooked! It was such a rush! Not just the TV part, but the *live* TV part! To me, there was something so exciting about the fact that I only had one shot to nail it—there were no do-overs or retakes.

The producers at *GMA* asked me to create a list of things that I was interested in or that I'd always dreamed of doing. So I started thinking about it, as lists like this are hard to make when you're put on the spot. Let's see . . . anything involving children, food, discount shopping, sports, animals, Derek Jeter, adventure parks and roller coasters, dance . . .

I figured that was a good start. I mean, what were the chances I'd actually get to do any of the things on my list, anyway? They were probably just trying to make me feel like I had a say in this process. Well, paint me red and call me cynical! Wouldn't you know that *GMA* made everything on my list happen!

Everything!

I got to go to the 2009 All-Star game and meet, yes, the man himself, Derek Jeter! Of course, by that point, Tye trumped even him, but STILL. I got to try out for the Rockettes. I got to ride roller coasters. I got to go discount clothes shopping! I mean, I got to do it all! And the best part of all? *This* was my job!!

fifteen

DREAMS REALLY DO COME TRUE

And then, on June 26, something happened that was the beginning of my real dreams coming true. The day certainly didn't start out that way. I was in a bad mood, and I mean a REALLY bad mood. I was trying to house hunt because I wanted to move somewhere closer to Tye. And although I was on my eighth week of looking, I couldn't find a house, and I couldn't get approved for a loan because I didn't have a job, and so I was incredibly frustrated with the whole process.

I had gone out on my own that day while Tye did some work at home. When I got back to his house, he tried to say hello and ask me about my day.

"Please stop talking to me," I said. "I'm in such a bad mood. This whole house thing isn't going to work out at all."

"Baby, it's okay," Tye said, while rubbing my shoulders and trying to be sweet to me. "Don't let today ruin it."

"Listen to me, Tye, just give me a minute," I said. "Let me have my time. Let me vent. Let me be in a bad mood."

I shut myself in his room and stayed in there watching TV. We were supposed to have dinner with his parents that night, but I didn't want to talk to anybody. I didn't want to do anything. Everything was annoying me. Tye came in, still being so nice about everything, even though I was in such a bear of a mood.

"We've got dinner with my parents tonight," he said. "Do you want to start getting ready? We can go early, and we'll just talk for a little bit."

I still was not in the mood to do anything or see anybody, but I could see that he was really trying his hardest.

"Yes, let's go," I said.

It was about a thirty-minute drive from his condo to his parents' house. On the way there, I started feeling better enough that I was talking and joking around some. Then, Tye drove past his parents' house.

"You just missed it," I said.

"Oh, they're not expecting us for another twenty minutes, so I want to show you something real quick," he said. "There's a church that, whenever we're married and we decide to move out this way, I'd like to maybe attend."

He stopped at this big church in Southlake, which is the town where he grew up and where his whole family lives. There was a small prayer chapel in front, and we got out and started walking up toward it. When we got inside, the air-conditioning wasn't working. This was Texas in June, so it was sweltering, and I couldn't figure out why we couldn't just talk in the car.

"It's awful hot in here," I said.

"Just sit down," he said.

So we sat down, and Tye started talking about his pop, who was his grandpa who had passed away. And then, he said the sweetest thing.

"I heard somewhere along the way that you'll know when you believe in angels because you'll see one in person," he said.

I just looked at him, and then I realized he was talking about me. He started kind of tearing up a little bit. And then, he had this little Bible in his hand and he read me a couple of Bible verses. I figured he was crying because he was talking about his pop, and I tried to comfort him.

"Babe, why are you crying?" I said. "Everything's okay."

We were sitting side by side, and then, he got in front of me, and I thought he was coming in for a hug, so I hugged him close.

But he pushed me away.

So I tried to pull him closer.

And he pushed me away more firmly.

I couldn't figure out why he was doing that when I was trying to make him feel better. He was struggling with something in his pocket. That's when I looked down and he had this squished up little ring bag in his hand.

I got it then, and I just stopped. We sat there for what felt like eight minutes, just staring at each other, and both staring at the ring.

"Melissa, will you marry me?" he said.

"Yes," I said.

I was just sitting there, crying and still looking at him and looking at the ring.

"Aren't you going to put it on?" he finally asked.

"You're supposed to put it on me," I said.

When he put the ring on my finger, it felt absolutely amazing. After everything we had been through, we had made it, and we were getting married.

After that, we went to dinner at a restaurant in Southlake. I knew that we were having dinner with his parents, but I didn't know that he had planned for my parents to be there, too. And then, we went to a bar downtown, and it was a total surprise because all of our friends were there to celebrate our engagement with us. When we walked in, everyone was standing there, clapping and screaming and yelling for us. It was one of the best nights of my life, and I had no idea how Tye pulled it off, no clue AT ALL that he planned this whole thing.

We had talked about getting engaged, so I had known it was coming, but I was never the type of person who made deadlines or insisted that I needed to be engaged by a certain point. I had told him that as long as I knew he was in this for the long run, I didn't need a ring right away. We had looked at them together a few times, but nothing serious. And let me say that just having him even look at a ring after a year and a half of dating, during which he never even saw my apartment, I knew that something was different this time around, and that we'd get there soon enough. I had figured I'd know when the time was near because he'd either be missing a lot or acting really shady and nervous, but I saw nothing coming. He had even thrown me off the scent by telling me he couldn't afford to get me a ring right then because he was putting all of his money into his agency. I was absolutely fine with that. Our life was so great as it was, and we'd technically only been back together for five months. But of course, when it happened, I was overjoyed.

All I had wanted for the past three years was to have Tye in this capacity in my life, and I was so happy that I felt like I needed to keep pinching myself. Tye and I both come from the belief that when you get married, that's it. There's no divorce, so you can't just change your mind if things get tough, and so it was the most amazing feeling to look at this man I loved so much and know that he was the person I was going to be with forever.

At least one of my friends was still wary about Tye when I told her the happy news. It actually took many of them a little while to trust him again. But once they saw how serious we were and had the chance to spend more time with him, they saw a different person and fell in love with him, too.

I know it's not completely accurate, but in my mind, I've only been proposed to once. And I've only been engaged once. Even though I believed in it at the time, I now look at the first proposal as something that wasn't real and only happened because I was wrapped up in this crazy television moment. I have, unfortunately, been engaged twice on paper. But I know how I felt when Tye proposed to me. And although I honestly can't remember what I was thinking when Jason proposed, I don't think it had anything to do with having found the man of my dreams, so much as elation that he had picked me. I have seen the clip of how I reacted when Jason proposed to me, and it was very showy, with him holding me and spinning me around, again and again, as the producers instructed us to do in order to get their shot. Tye's proposal couldn't have been more different, with just the two of us hugging and crying. As soon as I experienced that moment, I knew it was how it was supposed to be, and I knew, this time around, I had the right guy and it was going to be forever.

Life was pretty chaotic that summer. Tye was opening his agency and I was traveling more and more for *GMA,* plus appearances I had to do here and there. It started to cause a little bit of strain because, now, he couldn't travel with me anymore. So I quickly made the rule, with everybody who I work with, that I'm never gone from home for longer than four days. And if I am, then Tye needs a plane ticket, so he can come be with me. We've definitely turned things down because they didn't fit in with this schedule. But it's been worth it. There was a time when I was gone from home for too long, and as anybody who travels a lot knows, it's easy to lose it after a few too many hotel rooms. I reached a point where I just needed to go home. I needed to see my dogs. I needed to see my house. Plus, I knew it couldn't have been fun for Tye, when he was sitting in the office, working twelve-hour days, and then getting a call from me about how I got to meet Jennifer Lopez or visit the set of *Desperate Housewives,* or whatever crazy, amazing thing I did at work. But he was always so happy and supportive, and he got to come along on some fun adventures, too.

We planned our wedding quickly. We got engaged in June, and we were married by December. I guess that's nothing compared to getting engaged to Jason after three dates, but at least Tye and I had enough history to know that this was really going to last. The only reason it went that fast was that Tye was starting up his agency in the very beginning of January 2010, and so we figured we could either get married in six months, or we could wait a year and a half and do it after Tye had had the first year to get his agency up and running. Amazingly, after how reluctant Tye had been to make a commitment to me in the beginning, now he was actually the one who really didn't want to wait.

We didn't want anything big and extravagant, so we kept the planning low-key. I'm not an overly girly girl, so I'd never had a vision of a horse-drawn carriage or anything like that. But I had always been a hopeless romantic, and for me it was always just about being with that special person, and if that meant we went and eloped in Vegas, well, that was fine with me. When Tye and I did get engaged, I was coming right off *Dancing with the Stars,* and *GMA* had just started, so there was a big spotlight on me at that time. That public exposure made me want to try to keep our wedding as quiet as we possibly could.

Several different producers approached us, but after everything I had been through, I definitely didn't want to have a big TV wedding, or have taped clips of my ceremony running on an entertainment news show. I didn't mind taking pictures and putting them in a magazine, because I understood there was a demand for that, and we did sign a deal with *In Touch* magazine that they would get our wedding pictures. But they were very clear that if the paparazzi got pictures, then the deal was null and void.

All I wanted was Tye, our family and friends, and a beach. So we ended up running away to a little island, Isla Mujeres, in Mexico, and having it be as private as we could with about one hundred and seventy-five guests attending a small ceremony that both of our fathers performed.

We were on the island for a week before the wedding, and we could tell that we had drawn attention. We could just feel that people were looking at us, and we noticed there were people who passed by the house where we were staying again and again. Everything about the wedding was very casual. I didn't want anything stuffy. I told everyone not to wear shoes to the ceremony because we were on the beach. So everyone went barefoot, including me. Obviously that meant my dress was very casual too. I found this beautiful strapless, off-white Alfred Angelo dress that was tight around the top and tiered around the bottom. Tye wore a linen suit and he was barefoot, too. And handsome, of course.

Even though so many emotional ups and downs had proceeded this day, I was very calm before the wedding. My bridesmaids and I had rented a house, so we all got ready together. I had to take a little Pepto for my nerves, which I think everybody does. But by the time I got to the beach where we were having the ceremony, I was excited but relaxed.

And then, the music started. One by one, my bridesmaids walked away. The next thing I knew, it was just my dad and me. And then, they started playing, "Here Comes the Bride."

Oh my god, there's my cue, I thought.

My dad and I started walking. The anticipation of that moment was so built up, and so built up, that when it was my turn to come out, I got overwhelmed and I had to stop for a moment.

"Hold on just a second, Dad," I said, pulling him back.

My dad, of course, was crying. We started walking again, and I had these huge tears in my eyes. Then, I saw Tye, and he had these huge tears coming down his face. He's always said that it was really windy, and he just got sand in his eye. Yeah, right. But, in the moment, seeing how emotional he was made me feel even more emotional. I tried to keep my tears in check.

And then, as I walked down the aisle toward Tye, I was facing the ocean, and I could see a motorboat going back and forth. Someone was on board, snapping pictures. There were people who worked at the resort where we were, and they were all along the side of the guests, holding up mirrors. I had no idea what it meant, and as I reached Tye and stood next to him, he and I were cracking up because we were thinking that if our guests could have only seen what was going on behind them, they would have laughed, too. Then I realized that the resort employees were trying to reflect the light into the camera lenses, so it would be impossible for the paparazzi to take pictures, but it didn't work. They still got them. I looked at Tye.

"I can't believe we have paparazzi at the wedding," I said.

"You know what?" he said. "We're getting married, and you can either enjoy it or focus on the boat."

"You know what?" I said. "You're right."

My dad did a big opening prayer and spoke about the relationship between Tye and I, as he knew it. And then he sat down, and Tye's dad actually married us. Then, my dad said a few closing words, during which he started crying again, and Tye's dad pronounced us man and wife. I don't remember hearing a word of what they said except that we were now husband and wife, and that Tye could kiss his bride.

Oh, it's done, I thought. *It's done.*

Then, the paparazzi on the boat waved at us. And, just like that, they went away.

Tye and I walked back down the aisle to Monday Night Football's theme song, and then the party started. Our song, which we danced to during the reception, was "God Bless the Broken Road" by Rascal Flats. The lyrics very much fit us because it's all about wasting time going down the wrong path, but also being thankful for the broken road because if it weren't for that, we wouldn't be where we are right now. Yes, that was definitely our story.

The whole night was amazing, but the best part was that Tye and I had made it and we were together. We kept sneaking away, maybe five times during the night, to this huge dock that led out into the water. Each time, we hung our feet over the side of the dock into the water and turned around and took a mental snapshot of the whole fantastic party that was spread out over the beach.

"This is all for us," we kept saying.

After everything we had been through to get there, it was the best feeling in the world.

Our honeymoon was short, just two days in Riviera Mia, because we had to get back for the holidays and because Tye was really in the crunch time for his agency's opening. Later, we went back to Mexico over Valentine's Day for a really long weekend, and we kind

of called that our honeymoon. But, honestly, every single day felt
like a honeymoon to me.

I had decided that I didn't want to work at all over the holidays,
and then I got an offer that I just couldn't refuse. I had been invited
to cohost *Dick Clark's New Year's Rockin' Eve with Ryan Seacrest
2010*. It had always been a dream of mine to go to New York City
on New Year's Eve, because like everybody else in America, I had
watched that special and seen how magical it looked with the snow
and everything. I absolutely wanted to do it.

Tye and I went to New York City a week early for meetings.
And then, the morning of New Year's Eve, I did a *GMA* segment
from the top of the big ball that drops at midnight, which was
another one of the most amazing things I've done since becoming
a correspondent for the show. The only problem was that Tye and
I, both being from Texas, didn't know what a New York winter
felt like when we were packing for that trip. So I was wearing a
pair of jeans, my little knit gloves, and a jacket that was sufficient
in Dallas. But let's just say that in New York City, in December,
fifty stories up in the air, it was NOT enough. And then, it started
snowing. Tye and I couldn't believe how cold it was. And everybody
kept saying it was going to be a million times colder that night.
So he and I spent that whole day shopping, and when I assumed
my hosting duties that night, I was wearing something like four
layers of gloves, eight layers of tights and socks, plus I had heaters
everywhere.

As I was getting ready for the show, I actually started to feel
nervous, which was weird for me. We were in the dressing room,
and I knew we had about ten minutes before we went down, and
I started thinking about how big this show was and what a legend
Dick Clark was. And then, I was on my way down to where I

would be hosting from, and I met Dick Clark and his wife. They were so nice, and they knew who I was because they were fans of *Dancing with the Stars*. I couldn't believe it. I texted my dad right away: *I just met Dick Clark and he knew who I was! And he was such a great guy!*

When we got downstairs, it was total chaos. I don't know how many security guards Ryan had, but Tye and I had five around us. They had to push people away so I could get to my station. Where I was standing, it was a cameraman, two producers, and me. Oh, and a couple MILLION people who were there to celebrate. I was relying heavily on the producers to cue me as to when it was my time to go on because I couldn't see Ryan, and I had no teleprompter. I had in these earpieces that were supposed to allow me to hear the producers, but they didn't really work, because there was so much noise from the crowd. I realized I was going to have to just kind of wing it, and then I got REALLY nervous.

Faintly, I heard the music start in my ear. I knew we were going into the live broadcast, and then, it just flew by. It was the fastest three hours ever. When the ball dropped, Ryan was on, and I was supposed to go on after him. The ball was lowered, they started playing "New York, New York," and the confetti was flying. It was just this big, emotional high for me, and the tears started coming. Of course, then, I was the one on camera, and there I was crying, and I couldn't stop.

"I don't know why I'm crying," I said. "I'm so sorry. It's very emotional to be here."

This was my first New Year's Eve as Tye's wife, and that certainly would have warranted a kiss under normal circumstances. But the producers had initially said in all of the meetings that I shouldn't kiss Tye on camera because he wasn't going to be on camera other than that, and Ryan didn't have anybody to kiss. So I was fine with that. But then, when it actually happened, as I was crying and talking into the camera about what an emotional moment it was, I heard the producer in my ear.

"Kiss him, kiss him, kiss him!"

I wanted to talk back and remind them that they had told me not to, but I was on live TV, so I couldn't do that. Instead, I literally took Tye, grabbed him, and pulled him in, and we got our first married couple kiss of the new year on camera in New York.

The rest of the night didn't all go that smoothly, though. At one point, we were standing around, and the cameraman kind of just had the camera over his shoulder, and I was talking to an audience member. We hadn't gone over what my next talking point was because I knew we were still a little ways out from taping my next segment. And then, all of the sudden, I thought I heard the producer in my ear.

I had missed my cue and I was totally unprepared.

"Now what's going on with you, Melissa?"

"Um, um," was all I could get out.

The producers were looking at me, and then they started making a gesture for me to do something. The camera focused in on me, and I was standing there in Time's Square on New Year's Eve, LIVE, stuttering and having no idea what to do. I was still standing right by the audience member I'd been talking to, and so I turned and blamed it on this girl next to me.

"She just got me really flustered because she told me an inappropriate joke," I said. "I don't even know what to say. But I'm standing in Times' Square . . ."

I kept talking, trying to make it up as I went along, and I could feel myself sweating, even though it was about ten degrees outside.

It felt like the whole experience was at least three minutes long. My brain wasn't telling me what to do. I had no idea what I was supposed to say or where I was supposed to go afterward. *Do I shoot it back to Ryan? Do I go to commercial? What in the world do I do?*

Meanwhile, this poor girl next to me was looking at me like she couldn't understand what she had done to get singled out like that. FINALLY, we finished the segment, the camera went off, and I could breathe again. I had no idea what had just happened, and I thought I had ruined the entire show, and that the executive producers up in the studio were going to be so mad at me.

But, then, they came down and told me what had happened. Ryan had had a glitch, so he had to send it to me. And nobody had gotten the feed that it was coming to me, and so nobody had expected me to be prepared. Still, I felt bad and kept apologizing. The good news was that, even though it felt like an eternity, apparently, the whole thing had only lasted about twenty seconds. Even with that crash course in the potential drama of live television, the whole night was magic. Once again, it was one of those moments where I kept asking myself how I had gotten there, not only to live the dream of being in Times' Square for New Year's Eve with MY HUSBAND, TYE, but the fact that I wasn't even just in the midst of it all. I was out in this secure area, by myself, witnessing this amazing moment that meant so much to people all over the world. And then, afterward, I got to see Dick Clark again, and thank him, and see Ryan Seacrest again, and thank him, too. It was truly an awesome experience.

sixteen

MY REAL HAPPY ENDING

Tye and I were living in what almost felt like a weird fairy tale of a world, because everything we had both ever wished for had come true. Actually, wishes we didn't even know were possible were coming true. I used to always say that the best writers in the world could not have written our story and made it sound believable, because it was just too unbelievable.

Things were great on the home front. We bought our first house together. We had expanded our family by one puppy (he was a wedding present from Tye!). Tye had his agency up and running. I had my steady slew of jobs. Things were really, really good. We started talking about starting a family in the next couple of years. And where we wanted to end up: if we would stay in Dallas, or if we would ever move to LA, or at least get another house in LA. We loved playing the game of wondering where we would be in five years, and ten years, and twenty years. Basically, we were enjoying being newlyweds and having a lot of fun.

I loved being a *GMA* correspondent. It was literally like my dream job—making my living by traveling and meeting people— and I hoped I could do it forever. In early 2010 Deena called me and told me that she'd gotten a call from one of the producers for *Entertainment Tonight.* He told her he was a huge fan of mine and asked her if I'd want to come be a correspondent for sweeps week. He didn't have to ask twice. I was in. One of my first assignments was to cover the *Valentine's Day* movie premiere, which meant I got to meet Bradley Cooper and Julia Roberts. Um, absolutely! Count me in! It was a dream job—and a dream assignment! I was on the red carpet of a major movie premiere with some of the biggest movie stars around. I definitely didn't fit in, but I was having fun playing in their world!

Again, the stories I did for *ET* were fun and lighthearted, which is definitely what entertainment news is all about. And the more I did it, the more I found that it was really, truly my favorite thing to do. I realized that if I could pick my dream job, it would be doing some sort of entertainment news. Like I've said, I don't take myself too seriously, and I've never pretended that I could sit behind a news booth and give that kind of important information.

But becoming a correspondent for *Entertainment Tonight* and *The Insider* did come with some new challenges. As I learned when I did taped pieces for *GMA,* for some stupid reason, I get more nervous doing taped TV than I do with live TV. I know that's odd, because you would think, with live TV, it'd be easy for me to psyche myself out with the fact that it's LIVE TV. But I actually loved that feeling of only having that one shot, and having to think quickly on my feet—it kept things challenging and fun for me. Turn a live camera on me, and I'll perform without even thinking about it.

Of course, the first time I was on the set of *Entertainment Tonight,*

I found myself sitting up there with Mary Hart! She's a woman who is an absolute pro at her job, and it is *very* intimidating to be sitting next to someone like that! *Calm down, Melissa! You can't keep screwing up your lines; Mary doesn't want to sit on this stage with you for thirty minutes!* But it's definitely not as easy as it looks. I know from an audience perspective, it looks like anyone can look into a camera and talk, but there's actually a lot more that goes into it. You've got to know how to read a prompter (and how to make it sound like you're *not* reading), know what camera to look at and when, interact with the other person with you, be aware of your face, and nail the delivery. *Phew!*

My main problem has always been that I talk really fast naturally, let alone when I'm nervous. And so I knew every time I did a show like *Entertainment Tonight* that my note would be: *Do it again. Slow down.* I've learned to take deep breaths and count to three slowly in my head, to start a slower pace. Hey, whatever works, right?

I've found since working for *Entertainment Tonight* that I like to make fun of myself, and my situation, and laugh at people, and with people, and so having the chance to do that on the show was just the best. The job was supposed to last only through sweeps week, but then, the producers just kept bringing me back, one assignment at a time. They were linked with *The Insider,* and filmed on the same set, in fact, so they invited me to go start doing some stuff with them, which I also really enjoyed. What's not to enjoy?

I had the opportunity to cover the awards shows—both the Golden Globes and the Oscars—and it was just so unbelievable. I got to go to a showroom to try on dresses, and then get all dressed up and get my hair and makeup done, which for me was like being Cinderella. Normally, I'd be at home in my sweats all day, with my hair in a ponytail. After I got dressed up all fancy, and rode in the limo over to the theater, I found myself walking down the red carpet before the show started, with my shoes in my hand, to get to the place where the journalists stood.

The night that I covered the Oscars was a blur of the biggest celebrities, ever—Tom Hanks and George Clooney and everyone— and then I found myself talking to these people as if they were anyone else I might have met on the street. Never in my wildest dreams did I imagine that I would be interacting with Tom Cruise, and, surprisingly, I wasn't nervous at all. It was just fun. I kept reminding myself that they were just people. So when I talked with them, I didn't get quite as starstruck as I normally would have. I said *quite* as starstruck—I definitely still had stars in my eyes! I was so amazed that, a year ago, I had been a fan of these stars, and I had read about them in all the rag mags, and now I *knew* them. I'd talked with them. *And* it was documented on film that I'd talked with them. I really had!

By this point, with my personal and professional life both going so well, my time on *The Bachelor* began to feel very far away. I hadn't had any contact with Jason since we exchanged those few emails the night "After the Final Rose" taped, and I was just fine with that. When I looked back at my time with Jason, my conclusion was that it had never been a real relationship. I thought that it was at the time, I really did, but outside the Bachelor Bubble, I could see the truth of the situation. We went on three dates on the show. We didn't know each other well enough to know if we were in love or even compatible enough to get married. Afterward, because I had made this big, very public commitment, which I felt I needed to honor, I believed I really had to fight for my relationship with Jason. I actually think I fought harder for it than he did, especially if he had already realized that his heart was really with Molly. It was when I could tell that he wasn't going to reciprocate my efforts or my feelings that I finally gave up. I'm still not proud of that decision because I hate not seeing something through, especially something that important. But it's obvious that it never would have worked out.

I look back at how I've always felt about Tye, and then how I thought I felt about Jason, and it doesn't even compare. Tye has had my entire heart from the day I met him. So, in all honesty, Jason never really had a chance to steal my heart—because it belonged to someone else at the time. Even though I didn't know it, and I tried to deny it, it's the truth. And things ended up the way they should have: I married the love of my life, and Jason married the love of his life Molly.

And, yes, while Jason and I will always have this experience that bonds us, and we will always be associated together in the public eye—people to this day still come up to me and talk about how much they hate what he did to me. I've turned it around and can appreciate how much Jason helped me. Again, I wish it hadn't gone down that way, because of how it made me feel at the time. But it had to happen as it did for me to be where I am now. Not only professionally but personally as well. And I wouldn't change a single thing about how we ended up here.

Everyone seems to want me to feel this hatred toward Jason and Molly—him especially—and all of this anger toward both of them. But I just don't.

I *did*. Or at least I thought I did. But how could I ever be truly angry about something that ended up so great for everyone? We all hit potholes in life—and mine were definitely made public—but I'd do it all over again if it led me to the same outcome.

Looking back at the whole debacle I realized that I don't blame

Jason. Or Molly. It was going through the process and getting wrapped up in the behind-the-scenes maneuverings that led to a few lapses in judgment. But I don't think he's a bad person. I don't think she's a bad person. I've heard him say, even on that show, that he just followed his heart and did what was right for him. And I truly believe that. I don't think that he picked me just to dump me on TV and pick the other girl. And I don't think that Molly was the type of girl who deliberately set out to do everything she could to woo him away from me and win, after he had proposed to me. I don't think it was malicious. If I saw Molly somewhere tomorrow, I would talk to her. If I saw Jason, let's be honest, it would probably be awkward, but I wouldn't shun him. I do think she's a genuinely good person. I think he's a genuinely good guy. They both just got wrapped up in a really complicated situation, and, unfortunately, made a bad decision on national television that affected me positively and him negatively. I hate the way it happened. I absolutely hate it. I'm so embarrassed and humiliated, *still,* by the way it happened. And I know that to so many people, I will always be *that girl* who got dumped on *The Bachelor.* But I thank the Lord today for the way it happened. That moment literally changed everything in my life for the better, so if I had to go through that anger and embarrassment again to get to the joy and fulfillment that is my life today, that would be great by me. And I honestly do wish Jason and Molly both well.

That said, I've learned through all of this that I cherish my private life. I've seen what making it public can do, and I think that both Jason and Molly would admit that their lives were not easy for a long time because of the limelight. It's almost like their relationship was forced to survive because of how it all happened. A lot of people didn't believe in the relationship. A lot of people got mad at her for immediately taking him back, or got mad at him for dumping me, and then immediately making out with her on camera. But what I know from what I went through is that I'm sure the way it appeared on TV is not the way it really happened. I'm certain they had their own courtship, off camera, just like Tye and I did. I just don't happen to know it myself. And neither do the viewers.

But, again, reality TV has this way of airing what it wants you to believe. And as the viewers, we tend to believe it. This caused a lot of backlash against Jason and Molly, and a lot of bad tabloid stories with headlines like "Most Hated Bachelor Ever." I didn't envy them for that at all. I'm sure their relationship is probably a whole lot stronger for them having gone through that bad period. But from where I'm sitting, I know that I wouldn't want to put my relationship through that test. Tye and I have already been through the wringer, in part because of my time on reality TV, and if the only surefire way for me to guarantee that we're going to be okay is to not let people in too much, I'm okay with that. I'm happy to have a career on TV and leave my personal life back at home. I actually prefer it that way.

It was in January 2010, just after Tye and I got married, that I first heard that the production company Warner Horizon was developing a new show called *Bachelor Pad*. Now, these were the people who made *The Bachelor* and *The Bachelorette,* and who had tried so hard to convince me to be their next Bachelorette. And, apparently, ABC was interested in having me cohost the show. I heard a little bit about the concept, but not really in any great detail, and then, I stopped hearing about it. I got busy with *Entertainment Tonight, The Insider,* and *GMA,* and I figured the opportunity had gone away. Then in early May of that year, I received the news that the show was definitely on, and they did want me to cohost with Chris Harrison.

Wow! Really? What a great opportunity! I mean, first of all, it was a prime-time hosting gig. Those don't come along very often. Second, it was on network TV, which, again, is huge. And it was cohosting with Chris Harrison, who's a franchise name that's known by everyone. Careerwise, why would I not jump at an opportunity like that? I knew that the public might not understand why I would go back to a franchise that they felt did me wrong, but I didn't (and don't) feel like I had been done wrong by them. Again, I wouldn't even *have* a career in this industry if it weren't for them. So why the heck not give this a shot?

Come June, I moved out to LA again, for four weeks, to shoot *Bachelor Pad.* It was a crazy experience. I had never hosted a show before—and I had to do it alongside someone who had been hosting for years and years. Again, intimidated much? I basically just had to learn on the fly. I had a script to read, and tried to play off Chris and the contestants, but, again, it's harder than it looks. The producers have a clear vision of what they want the show to be, and it is my job to deliver. And it was extremely intimidating!

When we started filming, it definitely felt a little bit awkward because I had just gone through the whole process from the other side, and now they wanted me to be on their side—the production side—with Chris. It almost felt like I shouldn't be on their side because I wasn't above any of these contestants I had just been with. Technically, I should have been living in the mansion with all the other contestants, right? What made me qualified to stand up front with Chris and take on hosting duties? I had no idea, honestly. But I was up to the challenge and excited to learn.

My main concern was to not step on Chris Harrison's toes. This was, after all, *his* franchise. I wanted to find a place next to him that offered respect for the fact that he's been there for fifteen seasons now. Here I was, this little old contestant who was now a cohost, and I didn't want to overstep my boundaries. And to be honest, I struggled. It was the first time I'd ever hosted anything, and so I was learning how to work off the script while also making it my own. I was also trying hard to impress the producers—ironically, the same producers who had produced me a few years prior. Being the newbie on the set, I didn't want to disappoint anyone. Looking back, I would have brought more of my personality into it, but in the moment, I was terrified at every shoot we did. I just didn't want to mess up. When they needed me, I came in, said exactly what they wanted me to say, and tried to make friends and make amends that way. And I think it worked.

Once I relaxed, it was a fun experience. I got to see a lot of the girls I had lived with in the house and meet some of the new faces that had popped up in the past couple of years. *The Bachelor* franchise is really just like a big sorority or fraternity. Everybody from all of the different seasons knows one another. But I had been kept out of that loop because, after my season, I was busy working, and so I hadn't gone to any of the reunions. It was great to be on the other side of things and get to meet these people as friends now and not as competitors.

That was probably the strangest thing about the show, suddenly watching everything from behind the scenes, being in the control room with all eighty cameras, and hearing producers talk about all of the different backstories and why someone was crying. Meanwhile, I could look at that girl who was crying and know exactly how she felt. And even though the Rose Ceremonies were slightly different than they had been on *The Bachelor,* when I hosted them, I always sympathized with the girls because I knew how hard their hearts were pounding. It's been really exciting to have the chance to be in both positions; I think I'm the only person to have done that on the show.

Although it's easy for me to have perspective from where I stand, I know that if I went on one of these shows, even now, I would probably get wrapped up in it all over again. It's inevitable. They're set up in this certain way because it makes for good TV, and they'll always be set up in that way. So even though I sometimes found myself wanting to talk sense into one of the girls on the show, who had just met some guy and immediately thought she was totally in love with him, I never judged her, because I knew exactly where she were coming from.

You want to know my thoughts on reality television? Well, it's as real as you want it to be. As the viewer. As the contestant. Whoever you are and however you perceive it, I'll say it again: It's only as real as you want it to be. Take everything with a grain of salt and realize that behind the loveable good girl or malicious villain, there is a producer just trying to make a great TV show. And heck, they do, don't they? Don't judge what or who you see on the television set, because there most definitely is information that you're unaware of. Of course it's exciting to watch reality TV and pick the people who you love, or you hate, or you love to hate. That's part of the fun, right?

These days, many people go on the show to get TV time and become famous. I don't think these people will ever get their heart broken like I did because they're just in it for themselves. But there are those handful of people, every season, who are romantics like I was. I always feel for them when I watch them go through it, especially the girls, because they're always the ones who are so devastated when they get rejected. And I can totally understand why. It definitely makes me feel closer to them, having gone through it and been on the other side because, again, you can explain it all you want, but it won't really make sense unless someone has actually experienced it.

After Tye and I got married, we knew that we definitely wanted to have a semibig family, probably three kids, but we put ourselves on a three- to five-year plan. There were dreams I wanted to accomplish, places I wanted to go, and things I wanted to do. I'm Greek, and I'd always wanted to go to Greece. So Tye vowed that he'd take me to Greece before we had kids. We also planned to go backpacking through Europe and have all of the adventures we hadn't gotten to enjoy when we were dating because of everything else that was going on. At the same time, I wanted to see where this career would take me, and Tye wanted to build up his agency even more.

And then, as often happens, we were reminded that sometimes the universe has its own plans for how and when things will happen. About six months into our marriage, we found out that we were pregnant. It was a shock, but I suppose it's always a shock, whether you're planning or not. We looked at it as just another curveball we'd been thrown, and since we'd gotten pretty good at hitting those, and hitting them hard and far, we figured we'd be in good shape. And then we got really, truly happy in a way that was totally new and special for us.

Thankfully, my pregnancy didn't stop my career or change our lives at all. I was still been able to do what I do. Tye was still able to do what he does. We have such a great support system with both of our parents living nearby.

Tye and I made a pact pretty early on that our family would

always be the priority. As cool as my job is, and as many benefits as it brings, I'm not going to let it force me to give up any of what I've got at home. I would never take some multimillion-dollar deal if it meant I had to leave my family behind and go to LA. So far, Tye and I have been able to make it work by traveling out to LA a lot, usually together, and by sticking to that rule we made that we'll never spend more than four days apart at a time.

Home for Tye and me will always be Dallas, or at least wherever our families are. If I ever get the kind of deal that we just can't refuse, and we have to relocate to LA more permanently, I would not be surprised if our entire family moved with us, just because that's how important family is to us. As I have said, I do love what I do, but what keeps me grounded and keeps me sane are my home and my family. I mean, heck, we live in a house that is ten miles from my parents, two miles from his. It's in the same area where we both grew up. It's home. And I think when people lose their sense of that, they lose their sense of themselves.

The few times I have lived in LA, it's been fun. But it's not home. And it's a whole different world. People treat each other differently. And I can see why some people get very wrapped up in Hollywood and the paparazzi, and all of that. But I think it's important to remember that it's not normal. It is not normal to be followed to dinner by camera crews. And if a person who happens to be a TV personality starts getting in the mind-set that it is normal, and questioning why the paparazzi aren't outside the restaurant today, it becomes a problem. That's no way to live, especially because my career may go away, and I understand that. I look at how my career started, and let's face it, I am a reality star. I've gotten very lucky in the opportunities that I've had. But I'm not naïve enough to think I'm taken care of for life. It's not like now I'm Oprah Winfrey, and I am all set. I'm still on a gig-by-gig basis. I understand that I have to work very hard, and that even if I do, this may all go away.

But with everything as good as it is in my personal life, I'm honestly okay if that happens. I really am. A few years ago, I wouldn't have been. If the little bit that I had at that time had gone away, I would have been an emotional wreck. But I've grown so much, even just since then. And now that I've found the peace and happiness that I'd been looking for, I can see that it's really all I need. And so, I don't take any of it for granted. I love my life. I love what I do. But if it goes away, and I find myself teaching preschool in a few years, I'll be happy with that, too.

I think the most important thing I've learned from all of this, which I will take with me into whatever I do next—whether it's in the entertainment world or not—is the importance of being brave enough to take chances and try new things. When I look back, I see that if I had said no to *The Bachelor,* or no to *Dancing with the Stars,* which I considered doing in both cases, there's a chance that I'd still be at home in my cube, still single, and feeling like my life could be so much more.

But luckily for me, I had reached a point in my life where my motto, literally, was: *Why not?* The worst that can happen is that it won't work out. And that's okay. Just like I've learned it's okay to be rejected, and it's okay for some people not to like me. I can't please everyone. But if I do try something new, the benefits could be fantastic.

That said, I also know my limits. I've been lucky enough to get approached about all sorts of different things since *Dancing with the Stars.* I remember being very excited when I received a script to try to out for a part on a new sitcom. I was thinking how cool that would be. And then Tye and I read the script together, and I was practically blushing, just reading it. The character was overtly sexual, and I knew I couldn't do it. I can be goofy and silly. I can come in and be a ditz, but I can't do something that makes me embarrassed just thinking about it. Later, Tye and I watched the show, and it literally made me blush, so I guess I'm not the actress type. I mean, if I'm too immature to even read the script, that's not a good sign.

But I'm comfortable with my limitations, and I'm excited about everything that I *can* do. I can honestly say that I'm happier now than I've ever been in my life. And I feel really grateful. The bad times I went through definitely make me appreciate the good times now. And if I ever have little things to complain about in my life, I quickly take myself back to a few years ago and it sets me straight.

It's funny because there was a time in my life when it seemed like nothing would work out right. And then, starting with the time that everything made it so easy for me to go on *The Bachelor,* it seems like it all happened exactly as it was supposed to—even the parts of *The Bachelor* and "After the Final Rose" that I would have preferred not to have gone through.

Sometimes, even looking back from the place of happiness where I'm at now, it's hard to believe that I ever came out on the other side. Which is why it feels a little weird when people call me a role model. During everything I went through, I was just being me. I certainly didn't sign up to have influence and inspire people to follow my lead. But I have to figure that I must be doing something right if I'm having an impact on all of these women— and I don't only hear from a lot of teenage girls who are going through their first heartbreak but also from a lot of women my age, and even a lot of older women. To me, that's a huge compliment. If people can look at me and say, "I admire her because she went through this, and she came out the other end," that makes me feel really, really good.

Part of it is that I know that I'm not the only person who has suffered through heartbreak or public humiliation—or some combination of the two, like I did—and so I'm glad to give hope to those who are still in the early stages of dealing. You know, the stages of grief that involve a lot of tissues and couch time with good friends. But I also know that when you are weathering something rough, it's really hard to look at somebody that's happy, or that has successfully overcome his or her own tough times. For me, when I was heartbroken, I didn't want to hear my married friends tell me that it would get better. So the fact that people in the depths of their pain and misery are still contacting me, and can still relate to me without wanting to gag at my good fortune, makes me feel really proud and humbled.

That's why I decided to tell my story; to share what I've been through and how it shaped me into the person I am now, which is really the person I was all along. Only I didn't have the confidence back then to realize it. Also, I want to remind people that good times will be here again, even if it's hard to see that from the midst of a heartbreak. Believe me, I know the hardest thing to hear when you're heartbroken is that "time will heal all." But it's important to look back at the bad times and acknowledge them for the role they played in inspiring the kind of big, scary—but ultimately necessary—life changes we all need to make in order to get to the good times in our lives. Sometimes it's the disastrous work presentation that leads to the new, better job; the eviction that leads to the dream house; the nightmare breakup that leads to true love. And I truly believe that the bad times make you appreciate the good ones that much more.

I know it seems like it would be a lot easier to skip all of this bad, hard stuff. My best friends found love really easy. They didn't have to take the path I took. They got married at twenty-three, found the guys they were going to be with, and are still with them. I didn't have that. But a lot of other things did come easy to me. Whatever it is that challenges you, it forces you to grow up. It forces you to look around you and make do with what you've got. And it forces you to be grateful. Because no one is going to have a perfect life forever; I think it's written on our birth certificates that we're going to have hard times. And as hard as my hard times were, I would absolutely do it all again. I would feel that pain again, and I would cry myself to sleep if it led me to this outcome and the utter and complete completeness that I currently feel.

I cherish every good moment in my life right now, because I know there's a chance that it's not going to be this perfect again. But no matter what happens, I believe we all have a path to get to our happiness, whatever that is, and so if I do ever lose it, I will definitely find it again. And for right now, while I've got it, and I'm home in Dallas with Tye and our daughter, or traveling with them to do work that I love on *Good Morning America, Entertainment Tonight,* and *The Insider,* I want nothing more than to celebrate how I got here.

Because things lined up the way they did for Tye and me, we can't help but believe that some things are just meant to be. I feel like I've been living in a fairy tale for the past two years, and every time I look at my life and can't imagine it any better, it somehow surprises me and *does* get better. My biggest accomplishment of late is definitely the birth of our daughter, Ava Grace. And again, I'm looking at my life, and I don't know how it can get any better, but I know it will. Being at peace with my personal life makes everything else fall into place. I have my husband, my baby girl, and my puppies—I have so much love. I can't wait to see what the future holds for me, but I've become pretty good at expecting the unexpected.

And that's the real story of my reality—so far.

ACKNOWLEDGMENTS

I have to thank my husband, Tye, for everything that has happened in my life over the past several years. Odd as it sounds, I thank him for the person he was when we first met, and what we went through. If he hadn't broken my heart, my whole story wouldn't even exist. So thank you, Tye, for starting this crazy journey we've been on. And thank you for choosing me to spend the rest of your life with. Thank you for being my best friend. Thank you for giving me the greatest gift ever: our little girl. It's been a wild ride . . . it's been a crazy ride . . . but it's been a great ride. Thank you for being you, and loving me just the way I am. I love you.